Professional Boundaries in Social Work and Social Care

Professional Boundaries in Social Work and Social Care

A Practical Guide to Understanding, Maintaining and Managing Your Professional Boundaries

FRANK COOPER

Foreword by Jonathan Coe

Jessica Kingsley *Publishers*
London and Philadelphia

First published in 2012
by Jessica Kingsley Publishers
116 Pentonville Road
London N1 9JB, UK
and
400 Market Street, Suite 400
Philadelphia, PA 19106, USA

www.jkp.com

Copyright © Francis Cooper 2012
Foreword copyright © Jonathan Coe 2012

Library of Congress Cataloging in Publication Data
A CIP catalog record for this book is available from the Library of Congress

British Library Cataloguing in Publication Data
A CIP catalogue record for this book is available from the British Library

ISBN 978 1 84905 215 3
eISBN 978 0 85700 446 8

Printed and bound in Great Britain

Contents

Foreword

The creation of boundaries is at once a psychic necessity and an illusion. The need to draw lines allows for the existence of categories – this is this and not that – and, in this way, boundaries make thinking possible. We also establish rules that demarcate psychic space: don't touch me there, don't ask me that. However, there are no real lines, even on a physical level, just horizons where one entity meets another and the outer skin defines the borders between the two. In the psychic world, the lines are more blurry still. Who is to say where one's self ends and the other begins?

Andrea Celenza (2007)

The American psychoanalyst Andrea Celenza captures a central issue in thinking about professional boundaries – that they are both real and chimerical. Whilst there must be clear and unequivocal rules which outlaw some forms of behaviour (don't have sex with your clients, don't steal their money, etc.), in day-to-day practice most boundaries require reflection, thought and readjustment where necessary. Of critical importance is the need to be able to articulate any action, with colleagues and with supervisors, and to focus on the client's wellbeing as the trump card in choice-making.

One of my earliest memories is from 1971: my father bringing home a client of his, a young woman who had been prescribed Thalidomide during her pregnancy, and her daughter, whose crude prosthetics fascinated and alarmed us as we rolled around the floor together. Reflecting on this some 40 years later my father, the social worker, did not feel good about his decision to invite her into our home: 'What must she have thought?' he said.

Special treatment, and the urge to provide it, is one of the early warning signs that we teach practitioners to be aware of, part of a potential 'slippery slope' of behaviours which can lead to significant harm for clients, and professional disgrace for the practitioner. Frank Cooper provides helpful checklists and some core questions to assist practitioners in their decision-making.

Awareness of boundaries in professional practice has been around a long time, and they were memorably articulated by Hippocrates, in the Oath written in the fifth century BC. It included mention of staying within what one is trained to do: *I will not use the knife [...] but will withdraw in favour of such men as are engaged in this work.* It was clear on the need for confidentiality: *What I may see or hear in the course of treatment or even outside of the treatment in regard to the life of men, which on no account one must spread abroad, I will keep myself holding such things shameful to be spoken about.* And it outlawed improper relationships with clients: *Whatever houses I may visit, I will come for the benefit of the sick, remaining free of all intentional injustice, of all mischief and in particular of sexual relations with both female and male persons [...].*

But, as Cooper notes, there has been a dearth of education for social workers and there is no mandatory component on boundaries in formal social work qualifications.

Statutory regulation for qualified social workers has thrown a light on the previously hidden; we now know that significant numbers of cases coming before professional conduct panels have concerned violations of boundaries, in fact they represent one in five of all misconduct findings, a rate far in excess of figures published by, for example, the General Medical Council.

Boundary transgressions occur across all professions and the Clinic for Boundaries Studies is aware of cases involving hospital doctors, surgeons, complementary therapists, priests, psychoanalysts, counsellors and social workers. There appears to be a higher risk in disciplines which involve relationship as a central part of their practice. This may help to explain why there are significant numbers of cases within the talking therapies, why GPs and psychiatrists are reported more often than other doctors to the GMC and, perhaps, why social workers have seen such significant percentages in front of the Social Care Councils.

There are some dangers around the raising of awareness about professional boundaries. One is the overly rigid application of theory, a response which leads to organisational policies which make any self-disclosure by practitioners whatsoever (as one NHS

Trust has done) a disciplinary offence. Another is the idea that the boundary breachers are uniquely bad, nothing to do with the rest of the profession, and must be eliminated. In fact, boundary transgressions by intentional predators are much less common than those by 'ordinary' professionals and with this book Frank Cooper does much to improve professional understanding, and to protect the public.

Jonathan Coe
Managing Director, The Clinic for Boundary Studies
www.professionalboundaries.org.uk

Chapter 1

Introduction

What are professional boundaries?

Professional boundaries are a set of guidelines, expectations and rules which set the ethical and technical standards in the social care environment. They set limits for safe, acceptable and effective behaviour by workers.

The earliest known set of professional boundaries within Western society is the Hippocratic Oath. This was a code written in ancient Greece in roughly the fifth century BC and was intended as an ethical code for doctors and physicians. A translated and modernised version of the code is still used by some medical colleges around the world. The oath included, amongst other things, the following boundaries:

- You must understand the limits of your knowledge and not work beyond them.

- You must work with the good of the patient to the best of your ability and not do any harm to patients.

- You should not enter into sexual relations with anyone who has connection to your work.

- You should keep the details of your work with clients confidential.

Although the oath was directed at medical professionals, it featured many concepts that we use within the boundaries for social care professionals to this very day.

Modern professional boundaries are derived from a variety of sources. Some are from law or government papers, some are laid down and codified in quality standards, some are generally understood good practice, and some will be found in organisations' policies and procedures.

They are driven by many different factors: health and safety, therapeutic process, practical considerations, funding, client and worker safety. The result of this is that 'boundaries' is a catch-all term for a very varied collection of rules and guidelines.

Professional boundaries are not the same as the day-to-day boundaries/rules of your workplace. For example, many projects have a rule that clients must not attend whilst intoxicated. This rule is local policy and procedure, while the related professional boundaries would be that policy and procedure should be followed and enforced fairly and consistently.

Ultimately, being professional is about being good at your job and acting in a way that matches up with the expectations placed on you. Working in social work or social care, there is an expectation of responsibility that comes with the job.

As the worker you will always be in a position of power with respect to your clients. In most settings the worker will be thought of as the 'expert'. Clients will believe that you have the knowledge and experience to give your opinions authority. In most settings you will also literally have authority; you have a title, a place of work, other workers to support you and the right to refuse the client access to a service that they need or want. You may also provide a client with access to other services, funding or various forms of support or recognition.

All of these factors add up to putting you in a powerful position in relation to your clients. Clients will by definition be in need of some support and will often be vulnerable. Even if they are not vulnerable in any other setting, the power imbalance means that they are vulnerable in relation to you and your relationship with them. This puts you in a position of power and control, and with this power comes responsibility.

You will be expected to do the following:

- Help and support clients to the best of your ability and ensure that what you do does not harm them.

- Ensure that your actions are based around the needs of the clients wherever possible.

- Act in a trustworthy and responsible manner in all your dealings with and for clients.

- Be truthful and honest in your interactions with clients.

- Respect the clients' rights as individuals.

- Ensure that all current and potential clients have an equal opportunity to access and benefit from your service.

- Work for the good of your team and the organisation that you work for.

This means that your boundaries are not only about how you work with clients but extend to how you manage yourself and your emotions.

Managing boundaries is somewhat like walking a tightrope, trying to get a balance between various different elements. As a social care worker you need to be able to build up a good, close, trusting relationship with your clients whilst still maintaining a suitably professional detachment. The skill is learning where to draw the line.

Given the never-endingly complex nature of human nature, the line is ever-changing and you have to try to keep on top of it as best you can. It would be an impossible task to try to draw up a rule book that covers every possible situation. Each situation needs to be judged on its own merits. This book will lay out the guidelines and signposts that will help you draw the line in the right place.

Who is this book for?

This book is aimed at front-line workers delivering services to clients, or those training for similar roles. It is a basic introductory guide to the main issues that you need to have an understanding of.

The guidelines and boundaries within this book are intended to provide guidance for social work and social care professionals in a wide range of social care fields. The ideas and concepts are generic and can be applied across most sectors of social care. In addition, whilst teachers in schools and colleges are not generally seen as part of the social work and social care industry, these boundaries are also applicable to them.

The book is aimed primarily at those whose work involves talking to and supporting clients, rather than those involved in physical or medical therapies, although there is still much that could be learnt if you are involved in more physical hands-on work.

It is particularly suitable for workers in the following sectors: social work, homelessness/housing, addiction/drugs/alcohol, mental health, probation, youth work, supported housing and hostels, care homes, criminal justice, education, home care, care of the elderly, victim support, domestic violence, employment support and for key/support workers of all types.

The book works as an excellent primer if you are training to be a counsellor. However, if you are getting to Diploma level and intend to deliver intensive one-to-one therapy then the guidance will inevitably need supplementing with further reading which covers the issues around professional–client boundaries in greater depth.

If you work in private practice providing any kind of support and therapy, then it will be useful to you in terms of day-to-day working practice, but again, it is beyond the remit of this book to cover particular policy and procedures, insurance, supervision, and legal and ethical responsibilities.

As a generic book it does not deal with the specific application of boundaries in more specialist areas of work. Each sector will have its own ways of applying the concepts and each group of clients will have their own complications and needs. The sector and the setting that you work in will have an impact on how you apply the rules and guidelines given here.

If you have been working in the field for a long time and have experience and knowledge of boundaries, most areas discussed in this book should be familiar to you. However, reading it is a good chance to reflect on your practice. Dealing with your own boundaries is a constant process of awareness and you will still find something for you here.

Why write a book dedicated to boundaries?

Professional boundaries are the cornerstone of effective social care work. There may be some disagreement amongst professionals about exactly where to draw the line, but almost everyone agrees that a line needs to be drawn.

For such a vital area of knowledge, there is a remarkable lack of training and resources. There are many thousands of social care workers who are not trained counsellors but who have long, complex and deep professional relationships with their clients, dealing with a wide variety of issues.

Whilst anyone who has worked in social care for any time will know what boundaries are and will be dealing with them on a regular basis, it is amazing how few of us have had any formal training. Even trained social workers (who are more extensively trained than most) have frequently said they have not had such detailed information on professional boundaries.

Much of the deeper theory of boundaries comes from a counselling and psychotherapeutic background. Increasingly, social care workers in many roles are being required to deliver counselling style interventions, with aspects of cognitive behavioural therapy (CBT), motivational interviewing and solution-focused therapy being introduced. There are many workers going on short courses and then being expected to deliver relatively in-depth interventions without full counselling training, and therefore with a lack of boundaries training.

Organisations have increasingly sophisticated codes of conduct, so we have all been made aware of what the basic rules are. However, many codes of these focus on the broad issues and do not provide enough detail about the day-to-day dealing with boundaries.

Use of language

There are many debates about the correct terminology to use within the social care field. Given the wide-ranging scope of this book and its intended audience, there has been a need to make some decisions about what words to use. These decisions have been made for simplicity or because it is the language that feels most comfortable.

- *Social care.* This term is used in the book as a sweeping generalisation to cover many sectors and industries that provide support, care or advice to individuals or groups in need.

- *Support worker/social care worker/worker.* These terms are used loosely to describe anyone who interacts on a professional basis with individuals or groups who require care, support or advice.

- *Client.* This is a generic term for individuals who receive a service from a 'support/social care worker'. Other terms commonly used include service users, guests, pupils or tenants.

- *Relationship.* This term covers the interaction between a support worker and a client. The word does have obvious connotations (e.g. 'in a relationship' or 'having a relationship with'); however, it is the word that best encapsulates the nature of the interaction. The fact that there is a blurring between personal and professional illustrates exactly why boundaries are important in this setting.

Chapter 2

How Tight Are Your Boundaries?

The self-assessment questionnaire which forms the basis of this chapter is intended to get you to think about yourself, your clients and your behaviour before you read the rest of the book. The examples and the scores applied to the answers are intended to be representative examples, not cast-iron guidelines or rules. A good worker should judge every situation on its merit, which is why you need to think about boundaries so carefully.

For each question, choose one of the answers provided. There are of course many other courses of action you could take. Answer every question, trying not to think about it for too long. To make it a useful test you should put down the answer that relates most closely to how think you *would* behave, not how you think you *should* behave. There are no right and wrong answers, just more or less boundaried responses. You may want to choose more than one answer to some questions, but choose the answer that contains what you see as the most important response.

Once you have chosen all your answers, circle the numbers in the relevant lettered column on the scoring table then add up all the numbers that you have circled. Then compare your score with the scale following the scoring table.

Q1 You are walking with your partner and see a client you are currently working with, walking down the street towards you.

What do you do?

a. Ignore them.

b. Make eye contact and see what they want to do.

c. Nod a brief 'hello' to them.

d. Stop and chat with them.

e. Stop them and introduce your partner.

Q2 You are a live-in support worker at a residential project. One of your elderly clients turns up on your doorstep crying and upset late on a Saturday night.

What do you do?

a. Tell them you are off duty.

b. Ask them in for a quick cup of tea and a chat.

c. Escort them home and have a quick chat on the way.

d. Not answer the door.

e. Take them home, make them a cup of tea and get them to tell you what the problem is.

Q3 One of your clients notices you are reading a book by their favourite author. You have just finished the book and can tell they would love to read it.

What do you do?

a. Give them the book, as you have finished with it.

b. Hurriedly put the book away.

c. Discuss the ideas and themes of the book with them.

d. Suggest they join the local library.

e. Offer to lend them the book.

Q4 A client asks if you have a partner and children.

What do you do?

a. Give a totally honest answer.

b. Tell them it's none of their business.

c. Acknowledge your situation without giving too much information away.

d. Get out your family photos.

e. Have a moan about your partner/lack of partner.

Q5 One of your key clients who suffers from depression and is a heavy cannabis user is always late for your meetings, if they turn up at all.

What do you do?

a. Keep offering them appointments and do the best you can.

b. Make extra effort to remind them about the appointments.

c. Offer to make home visits.

d. Tell them they need to turn up or the sessions will end.

e. Spend the session looking at their inability to turn up on time.

f. Try to devise an action plan with them to deal with the issue.

g. Tell them that when you smoked cannabis it made you lazy as well.

Q6 A client who you have been working with stops engaging with you and rejects your attempts to support them.

a) How do you feel?

a. Sad.

b. Annoyed.

c. Disappointed.

d. Angry.

e. Nothing, they're just a client.

b) What do you do?

a. Let them know you are there for them whenever they are ready.

b. Tell them how shut out you feel and that they have let you down by rejecting you.

    c. Get another worker to try to talk with them.

    d. Leave them alone until they decide to engage.

Q7   A client tells you that you really 'get' them and no one else understands them, and that they think you are a wonderful person.

What do you do?

    a. Thank them and say that they are a special person.

    b. Act pleased but modest.

    c. Explain that you are just doing your job.

    d. Tell them to stop being soft.

    e. Give them a hug.

Q8   A client gets engaged and says that they will invite you to the wedding and that they would really like you to be there after all you have been through together.

What do you do?

    a. Say you will start looking for an outfit.

    b. Tell them that you don't think it is appropriate for you to go.

    c. Tell them you would love to come but professional boundaries mean that you can't.

    d. Be vague, intending not to come anyway.

Q9   You are working with an ill elderly client. They become too ill to do the shopping and at the end of one session they ask you to pop to the shops for them as they have no food in the house. It is outside of your job description and hours of work.

What do you do?

    a. Take the money offered and go to the shops for them.

    b. Say you are unable to go for them.

    c. Offer to do the shopping on a regular basis for them.

    d. Ring your organisation and get clearance to do the shopping.

Q10 You are working with a client who you believe is becoming sexually attracted to you. They flirt mildly with you in one-to-one sessions.

What do you do?

a. Speak to your supervisor/manager about the situation.

b. Play along with them so you don't hurt their feelings.

c. Tell them that this is a professional relationship and that they should not be so over-friendly.

d. Get them transferred to another worker.

e. Stop booking one-to-one sessions with them.

f. Book a home visit to discuss the situation.

Q11 One of your clients is a financial advisor. Whilst chatting they tell you about some stocks and shares you should buy now to make lots of money. You do currently have some money you are looking to invest.

What do you do?

a. Tell them that you are here to advise them, not the other way round.

b. Tell them you don't invest in the stock market, but follow their advice secretly.

c. Be polite but disinterested and ignore the advice.

d. Ask them for more details so you can check it out later.

Q12 A new client spontaneously gives you a hug at the end of a particularly good session.

What do you do?

a. Hug them back and tell them what a positive session it was.

b. Let them hug you but don't really engage.

c. Avoid the hug and tell them it is not appropriate.

d. Accept the hug and tell them it is not appropriate.

e. Tell them not to ever touch you.

Q13 A volunteer working with the project seems slightly out of sorts and you think you can smell alcohol on them, although you are not sure.

What do you do?

a. Keep an eye them and act if their behaviour is wrong.

b. Ask them if they are feeling all right.

c. Ask them if they have been drinking.

d. Explain your concerns and the reasons for your concern.

e. Speak to your manager.

Q14 You turn up for a home visit and the client answers the door wrapped in a towel.

What do you do?

a. Refuse to enter the house and walk away.

b. Tell them to put some clothes on and wait outside whilst they do.

c. Laugh it off and go in anyway.

d. Suggest they need to put some clothes on before starting the session.

Q15 You turn up to meet your friends for a drink in the pub. You see one of your current clients in the pub with some of their friends. The client looks slightly drunk.

What do you do?

a. Ignore your client all night.

b. Speak to your client and suggest they leave the pub.

c. Ask your friends to leave with you to another pub.

d. Have a word with your client and suggest that you ignore each other.

e. Buy your client a drink.

Q16 One of your clients brings you a reasonably expensive bottle of perfume/aftershave as a gift towards the end of your time working with them.

What do you do?

a. Accept the gift with thanks.

b. Refuse the gift as inappropriate.

c. Accept the gift but say you will have to share it with the team.

Q17 Whilst chatting with a client, they mention your favourite band/musician/singer, saying how much they love them.

What do you do?

a. Listen and ask them questions.

b. Say how much you like the artist.

c. Start chatting in depth about the music/lyrics.

d. Talk about the time you saw them play live.

e. Change the topic of conversation.

Q18 You are chatting with a group of clients when one of them tells a mildly racist joke. All the other clients laugh and you think the joke, although tasteless, is quite funny.

What do you do?

a. Smile to yourself but walk away.

b. Keep a straight face and say nothing.

c. Challenge the clients directly about the implicit racism.

d. Say that you find the joke offensive.

e. Remind them of the rules about racist language.

f. Laugh (but not too loud).

How tight are your boundaries? Scoring table

	A	B	C	D	E	F	G
Q1	1	2	3	4	5		
Q2	2	4	3	1	4		
Q3	4	1	3	2	4		
Q4	3	1	2	4	5		
Q5	3	3	4	1	2	2	5
Q6a	3	3	3	5	1		
Q6b	2	4	2	3			
Q7	4	3	2	1	5		
Q8	5	2	4	3			
Q9	3	1	4	2			
Q10	3	4	2	1	2	5	
Q11	1	3	2	5			
Q12	4	3	2	3	1		
Q13	4	3	1	2	2		
Q14	1	2	5	3			
Q15	4	1	2	3	5		
Q16	4	1	3				
Q17	2	3	4	5	1		
Q18	3	4	2	2	2	5	

Total score _____

22–35

Your boundaries are very severe, you should loosen up a bit and try and see things from your clients' point of view.

36–56

You're nice and safe, no problems. You could stretch yourself and with careful consideration you could work a bit closer to the line.

57–75

You are treading a fine line between boundaried and unboundaried behaviour, though if you do it with enough consideration, judgement and caution you will be fine. If you are not careful enough you will cause problems for yourself, your team or your clients.

76–80

Your boundaries are very loose. You are setting yourself or your clients up to fail. Have a good think about your motivations and personal boundaries.

81–88

Your boundaries are non-existent. You need to sharpen up fast before you cause some serious problems.

Commentary on the self-assessment questionnaire

Below you will find a brief explanation of the issues raised by the questionnaire.

Q1   It is important not to engage too much with clients outside of work; however, if you blatantly ignore them they may be offended. Do also remember that they may not wish to see you outside of work either, so allow them their anonymity if they wish. They may not want friends or family to know that they receive any kind of support or professional help.

Q2   As a live-in support worker it is important that you have some time off. If you give residents time outside of your normal hours on a regular basis you will find that your time off will get used up more and more. If there is a genuine emergency then you may just have to sacrifice your personal time. However, residents should learn to come to you with problems within your work time. If you do wish to give them some TLC, then doing it as you walk them home is a simple way to control the interaction and allow yourself a polite way to end it.

Q3   Lending someone a book may seem fairly harmless, but it is the giving of a gift and it is not something you will do with every client. You do need to assume that any book that is lent may not come back and if the client loses or damages the book they may feel bad about it and this may impact on your ability to work with them. If they are interested in reading then this is a cue for you to encourage them to pursue this interest, not a cue for you to deepen your relationship with them.

Q4   If you have a long relationship with a client then they will probably find out some of your personal circumstances. The basic facts about your personal life do not need to be totally guarded secrets. You should ask yourself why they are asking the question, what your motivation is for your answer and what they might do with the information.

Q5   On the one hand you should try to understand your clients' issues/needs and make adjustments to the service you provide accordingly. On the other hand you should not enable or reinforce their negative behaviour or disempower them by doing all the work for them.

Q6   There is nothing wrong with having feelings about your client's behaviour; however, you must realise that these are your personal feelings and should not influence your professional judgement. It is acceptable to acknowledge your emotions to your client in a controlled and professional way.

Q7   Whilst this statement clearly shows that you are doing some things right, it should also serve as a warning signal that this client is putting you on a pedestal or becoming over-dependent on you. You should not feed into and encourage this behaviour but you should not reject it either.

Q8   Going to someone's wedding is clearly a very personal matter and should be avoided if possible. If it is very appropriate to go then you could go with another member of staff and attend the ceremony but not the reception. Remember not to hide behind the rules when rejecting the invitation.

Q9   If there is no other suitable option then you may sometimes feel you must cross professional boundaries; however, make sure that you contact your line manager/organisation and watch out for problems relating to handling clients' money. Ensure in cases like this that you try to set up some suitable ongoing support to ensure the situation does not occur again. You must also explain to the client clearly why you are doing what you are doing.

Q10   Some mildly inappropriate behaviour does not mean that you have to end a relationship, although you should challenge the behaviour. This may be unthinking behaviour or a common pattern of behaviour for this client. You should always report this sort of issue to a line manager and/or make sure that your case-notes clearly mention it. It is easy for clients to feel rejected in this situation so you should handle it carefully.

Q11   Your sessions with clients should focus on their issues and concerns, not your finances. If you followed your client's advice (even secretly) and lost a lot of money what impact would it have on your relationship with them?

Q12   Hugs are a sign of a close physical relationship and should be avoided wherever possible as they may give your client, or other clients, the wrong idea. Sometimes it is impossible to avoid a hug – it may be difficult or hurtful to physically push the client away. In these cases you should accept the hug with the minimum contact and then explain that it is inappropriate for you to hug as you need to keep the relationship on a professional basis.

Q13   If you suspect that there is an issue with another member of staff (paid or voluntary) it is your responsibility to do something about it. If there is a problem later that day and you kept quiet then you share responsibility for that problem.

Q14 Clearly, being in a closed space with a client wearing only a towel should be avoided wherever possible. There are obvious issues around sex and nudity and you are there to have a professional relationship and appropriate clothing should be worn by each side.

Q15 You may sometimes encounter clients outside of work. It is best to leave these situations if at all possible. Be aware that in a pub environment you may both be slightly intoxicated and this increases the risk of difficulties. Even if you avoid each other you may have to use the same toilet facilities or bump into each other as you leave at the end of the night.

Q16 There are obvious problems with accepting gifts. Perfume can be quite expensive and is something that it is not so easy to 'share with the team'. Even though the client is leaving there are still potential repercussions from accepting a gift.

Q17 Music is something quite personal and something that you indulge in when you are outside of work. A shared love of music can bond people very quickly. This information is a chance to understand your client more, not a good issue to bond with them over. Your client should like you because you are a good worker, not because of the music that you like.

Q18 Clearly, racist behaviour of any sort needs to be challenged; even a small level of indulgence of it can act as permission to behave in that way in the future.

Chapter 3

Why Do We Have Boundaries?

The big picture

Boundaries underlie almost everything that we do within social work and exist to protect everyone involved. At the broadest level it can be said that the entire population has some involvement with or reliance on social work.

If you look at the bigger picture, all of the groups below should expect that a safe, professional and effective service is delivered by social care professionals. Each group needs to be protected, in different ways, from abuse, negligence or self-harm:

- *Clients: individuals who receive a service from workers and organisations.* Clients can be abused by other clients or by workers, can suffer as a result of negligent workers or organisations and often need to be protected from themselves or the consequences of their behaviour.

- *Workers: the staff who manage and deliver the services to clients.* Workers can be abused by their clients or other workers, can suffer as a result of the negligence of their team members or organisations and need to be protected from burning themselves out or from the consequences when things go wrong.

- *Organisations: charities, business and government organisations that employ and manage the workers.* Organisations can suffer if their employees or clients are abused by each other, can suffer legal consequences as a result of negligence and need to understand their responsibilities to their workers and clients.

- *Funders/stakeholders: organisations, charities, local councils and government departments that provide the money to organisations.* Stakeholders need to know that their money is being well spent, that they are not paying for abusive or negligent services and that appropriate outputs and outcomes are achieved.

- *The wider community: anyone whose life could be impacted on directly or indirectly by the services that are offered.* The wider community relies on the support services to protect and support themselves, friends, family and their neighbours and the community in general.

Therefore all of these groups rely on the quality of the service provided by the workers to the clients. The quality of this service is determined by the ability of the staff and managers to work within their professional boundaries.

The specifics

To establish a safe, supportive relationship

Many of the boundaries that apply to workers' behaviour help to create a safe, open, stable, transparent relationship that is clearly based on the client's needs. If a client understands what will or won't happen in given circumstances it gives them a sense of control. If the purpose of the relationship, the role that worker and client play, and the rules that govern it are clear, then the client can relax.

Change and uncertainty create anxiety and no one is at their best when they are anxious. Whether you want to make a client feel comfortable with you supporting them in their own home, or comfortable enough to explore difficult personal issues, boundaries provide a safe framework.

To ensure good practice and minimum standards

It is important for any profession to be able to set out the standards for its members. This enables us to lay out clearly what is expected of workers and organisations and provides something to measure and evaluate them against.

To build and maintain client trust

As individuals and as a profession we rely on our clients trusting us. Clients do place an amazing amount of trust in us, letting us into their lives, their homes and their families.

Nonetheless, clients will often group all social care workers together in the same bracket, and will have certain expectations, judgements and beliefs about us. If we break boundaries and abuse clients' trust in us it will rebound not just on us and our relationship with that client. It can impact on that client's trust and engagement with services in general and can colour other people's opinion of the profession.

Have a think about how much harm the Victoria Climbié case did for the reputation of social workers, or what Harold Shipman did for the relationship between older patients and their doctors. Imagine how you would feel having had your trust betrayed, and how hard it would be to re-engage with a similar situation to that which led to the betrayal in the first place.

To ensure consistent service delivery

Boundaries ensure consistency between team members and between different professionals. Being a client of social care services can be a difficult and confusing journey, particularly if with different services and workers. It helps clients if they know roughly what they can expect when they see a professional care worker.

To ensure team coherence

Workers need to work together as a team and provide a united front, all working towards a common goal in a common direction. Having boundaries allows for individual working styles and personalities whilst maintaining a unified approach. It is very easy for teams to become split and manipulated by clients if their boundaries are not tight.

To provide a framework for the relationship

The relationship between workers and clients can be very fluid and dynamic, changing constantly. Fixed boundaries and ways of working provide a safe framework for this relationship to exist in. For both worker and client, having some fixed points, some guidelines and some certainty in at least some areas is useful.

To set the limits between clients and workers

Boundaries help both clients and workers understand their respective roles. Interpersonal relationships can get complicated in any setting and when you are working with vulnerable individuals especially so. There are different expectations of behaviour for clients and workers. Boundaries draw a line between workers and clients. This line is there to keep each side safe.

To keep the relationship on a professional level

It is very important for a wide variety of reasons to keep the relationship between clients and workers on a professional level. With the in-depth nature of the relationship and the personal nature of some of the work that is done it would be easy for the relationship to slip into a personal one.

To avoid feeding into clients' vulnerability

Many clients who present to social care services will have had previous bad experiences of being abused and victimised. This can leave them with low self-esteem and little status and power in society. These clients are very vulnerable to abuse as they can be overly reliant upon the opinion of others. Never underestimate the impact that your words and actions can have on vulnerable clients. For someone in this position it can be very easy for inappropriate behaviour by the worker to feed into previous patterns of victimisation and boundary pushing.

To ensure health and safety

Boundaries ensure the health and safety of workers and clients and in particular help ensure that workers take responsibility for maintaining that safety. On a very obvious level there are rules relating to safety (fire policies, lone working, etc.), and it is every worker's professional responsibility to ensure that they work within these rules.

On a slightly less obvious note, how workers manage basic boundaries on a day-to-day level affects the general level of safety of their place of work. If basic boundaries are not maintained it is much more likely that incidents that are dangerous (physically and mentally) for both staff and clients will occur.

To prevent burnout

Social care work can be very demanding for the workers – dealing with other people's emotions, crises and problems on a daily basis can be very draining. If you allow yourself to become too involved with your clients' issues and take too much of your work on board, or home with you, you can become drained, cynical or over-involved. You should be able to have a long and happy career in social care if you look after yourself. Remember, if you can't look after yourself, you won't be much help to other people. You have a responsibility to support all your clients to the best of your ability. Boundaries help you to maintain a close and supportive relationship without becoming too personally involved.

To minimise misunderstanding

Clients who have low self-esteem, anxiety, depression or who are generally vulnerable can be very sensitive to a level that you would not normally expect. They are very likely to have negative thought patterns and negative beliefs about themselves and how other people see them and treat them. It is important therefore to be very careful about how you act and what you say. Boundaries provide guidelines to ensure that workers do not harm clients unintentionally by the way they act.

To teach boundaries

Many clients who are in the social care system suffer from a lack of boundaries. They may have trouble maintaining personal boundaries if they suffer from an addiction. If they have had poor parenting they may not understand what a boundaried relationship is. Clients who break the law have a problem dealing with some of the basic norms and boundaries of society. People who have been hurt or abused will often act out their feelings and push or ignore boundaries pathologically. Much social care work centres around teaching boundaries to clients or helping them to manage personal boundaries. If we cannot demonstrate some personal and professional boundaries to them, it will be very hard to support them.

To provide a role model for clients

Even on a day-to-day basis, we require boundaried behaviour from our clients just to engage with our service. They mostly have to turn up on time, not be too intoxicated, be able to control their emotional reactions to a certain extent, and abide by rules of equality and diversity whilst in our projects/offices. People respond to the behaviour that they see around them and will treat you accordingly. If you act chaotically then your clients will be more chaotic. If you are aggressive you will get back more aggressive behaviour. If you maintain good boundaries you will get a more boundaried response from your clients. That is not to say that they will not cross or push at boundaries, particularly at first, but eventually most clients will settle down if you are consistent.

To ensure equality of access

Professional boundaries help ensure that any social care services are safe and welcoming places for everyone. For further information see Chapter 7, 'Professional Boundaries and the Law'.

To reduce the risk of client exploitation/abuse

Abuse of clients by workers is not the norm, but is still more common than one would hope or expect. Having standards that we can be held accountable to and a common understanding of good practice does help to minimise abuse. It also provides a framework for disciplinary matters that enables us as a profession to deal with the perpetrators. Clients are very vulnerable to abuse by professionals that they depend on and they may not understand professional boundaries in detail. Having some consistency in approach does help them identify if they are being poorly treated. This lack of understanding of boundaries (both professional and otherwise) means that social care clients can be particularly vulnerable to abuse and therefore rules and regulations are required.

Many situations where a client is being abused by a worker will slowly slide from being a suitable, professional relationship into being an abusive relationship. The slide is facilitated by a number of smaller boundaries being crossed along the way. This is either a worker 'grooming' a client or a misguided worker getting drawn into a situation where they are out of their depth or out of control. Having some basic standards and boundaries does help spot the 'grooming' and provides guidance for those who may slip up.

To prevent role confusion

It is very easy for clients to become confused about the nature of the relationship and, for example, to imagine that a worker is their friend, or to put them into a parental role in their life. Working within your boundaries minimises the chance of this happening.

To build independence

It is the aim of almost all social care roles to encourage clients to be as independent as possible. Different clients will be able to achieve different levels of independence depending on the issues they face in life.

If clients did not need support in some way then they would not be accessing social care services. If our service did not meet their needs then we would be failing them. It is natural to a certain extent to become dependent on a service or a worker that meets your needs. If clients are feeling low in spirit and energy they may happily pass over responsibility for managing their life to others. Without boundaries to guide workers and organisations we would see a much greater level of client dependence on services.

To empower clients

Maintaining a compassionate, boundaried approach ensures that we do not disempower our clients by the very act of supporting them. It is very easy to support someone too much or to act in a way that undermines their self-esteem and motivation. By doing too much work for the client or making them feel better you can make them emotionally dependent on you.

To provide professional detachment/objectivity

The advantage of working with a professional is that they have the detachment to stand back and see the bigger picture. If your relationship becomes too involved you may lose that oversight and focus. If you lose that focus, your judgement is clouded and you will be of less use to your clients.

To maintain focus

Even with the particular role or job clearly in mind, it is easy to become distracted or lost within your work. Many clients have chaotic lives, chaotic minds or have physical, mental or social issues that encourage chaotic unfocused behaviour. As professionals, our job is to maintain a professional focus and reach or head towards certain goals.

Even with a very compliant and focused client, it is easy for workers to wander off the track and overstep their role, becoming nosey or over-involved in areas that are not their focus. Boundaries are the guiding principles that help to keep us heading in the right direction at all times.

To manage clients' behaviour assertively

In most settings there is some aspect of managing clients' behaviour involved in the work. It is important that this is done respectfully and without damaging the positive relationship that you need with your clients. It is important that workers retain control of their emotions and behaviour, particularly when working with challenging clients.

Having professional boundaries helps us to manage this process and to ensure that it is done correctly. They provide a guideline for staff and also help staff to remain professionally detached so that they can remain calm and focused.

To minimise clients mirroring personal behaviour/feelings

When you work with a client for a period of time it is natural that some synchronicity of thoughts and feelings may occur. You will find that you will be feeling the same feelings at the same time. With some self-awareness this can be a useful tool for a worker because it can give you an insight into the mind of the client.

However, if the client is picking up too much of your personal feelings that are not related to the work, it can cause problems for them. Acting in a boundaried way does not eliminate mirroring but it will minimise it, especially in relation to personal issues that are not relevant in a work setting.

Why worry about these details?

It may appear that worrying so much about all of these boundaries all of the time is very pedantic and unnecessary. Some people feel that as long as you don't actively abuse the clients then everything is fine.

However, there are a number of golden rules of boundaries that mean that you need to look after the details and the basic day-to-day boundaries, so that you don't encounter so many big, frightening boundary crossings.

1. It is much harder to maintain boundaries when boundaries have previously been crossed

If a particular boundary has been crossed, or if there is generally a poor standard of boundary management, it takes more effort to enforce it and enforcing it will cause many more problems in the short term. This is true for both individuals and teams. Each time a boundary is not maintained the authority, confidence and ability of the team, or individual, are all undermined.

If a client or client group is used to boundaries not being maintained then there is a hugely increased chance of them reacting badly when boundaries are enforced. When boundaries are first enforced there is a natural reaction for people to kick against them. The boundary crossing behaviour will probably intensify in an effort to restore things to the previous status quo. If boundaries are maintained consistently in the face of this behaviour it will end. (For a 'by-the-book' illustration of this behaviour watch any of the nannying/parenting shows that are on TV.)

2. People sense and react to the boundaries in an environment

Clients will be able to tell very quickly, consciously and subconsciously, what are the boundaries of an organisation, project or worker. We all get a feeling for a place or a person quite quickly, from our experience, from what we see around us and from our intuition. We can quickly get a feel of whether somewhere or someone is organised, efficient, and well managed, or whether disorganised and lax. We can get a sense of whether rules are obeyed or whether corners are cut. Even if we don't consciously acknowledge the fact, it will be taken on board and we will start to modify our behaviour.

If we sense that somewhere is boundaried and efficient, then we are less likely to try and push the boundaries. However, if we sense that boundaries do not really matter then we are more likely to behave in boundary crossing ways.

Breaking boundaries

When a client arrives for their first appointment the worker they are there to see is late. The waiting room is dirty and has racist graffiti on the walls. While they wait they see clients arguing and swearing. When the worker comes out to meet them he gives one of the clients a friendly hug, and explains his lateness by moaning about other members of staff. During the session the worker answers his mobile phone and then tells the client about the health problems his wife was telling him about on the phone. They get on well but the worker appears to be flirting and joking with the client. When he hands over an information sheet it has the front sheet of another client's assessment stuck to it.

The first question is whether the client will stick around or have any faith or trust in the service. If they do, they will react to the behaviour of those around them. Depending on the client's personality they will either feel unsafe and clam up to protect themselves or feel that they can do what they want. In either case they are much more likely to push or break boundaries in that environment.

To use an analogy, imagine you were driving in a new country.

If everyone drove very slowly, very calmly in straight lines and waited patiently at traffic lights, the rules of the road were clearly marked and signposted, and if anyone broke the rules they were swiftly stopped by the police, how would you drive? On the other hand, if everyone swerved and beeped and drove like maniacs, ignored red lights, and drove on the wrong side of the road, how would you drive?

In either case, whatever your natural driving style you would tend towards the local driving style. Partly because you would have to do so to get by on the roads and partly because you would mirror the other people.

3. Major boundary crossings are almost always preceded by a series of minor boundary crossings

Boundary crossings are very rarely isolated events – they mostly happen within the context of a relationship between two people or a group of people. This history and dynamic of the relationships set the tone and the background for the crossing.

If you look into any case where a major boundary has been crossed by a worker, there will be a series of seemingly less serious boundary crossings that build up to it.

In the case of a sexual relationship between a client and a worker, there will have been joking and mildly flirtatious behaviour, an increase in minor physical touch (a squeeze of a hand or a touch on the shoulder), a rule may have been bent and some extra work done for the client, time will have been spent chatting socially, personal information shared by the worker, a meeting will be arranged outside of normal work hours and then the first kiss will happen.

The same is true of major incidents in a social care service. Once you look at the reasons for a serious incident occurring and start analysing the build-up to the incident you will see that a number of boundaries will have been crossed. These crossed boundaries will mean that opportunities to take action to avoid the incident will have been missed.

In the case of a physical attack on a worker by a client, perhaps a worker will forget to hand over to anyone the fact that the client has suffered a loss in the family. Another worker spots that the client is in a bad mood but is too busy concentrating on their favourite client. A key work session is cancelled by the worker in question without any notice and an argument involving the client is dealt with unfairly. At the end of the day the worker challenges the client on why they did not participate in a group activity and the client lashes out.

If you look at any of the highly publicised cases of death of young children who were known to social services, all of the investigations have shown a whole series of broken boundaries by many organisations involved in the case.

4. You can never really tell how a situation will unfold

With the best will in the world and hours of analysis, you can never really predict how people will react and how a thing will play out from any given situation. As you become more experienced as a worker you can start to make better and better guesses at how things will turn out. But even when you predict correctly more often than not, you are still relying on assumptions and guesswork which may prove to be incorrect.

This unpredictability means that you need to ensure that your house is in order and everything is as secure and boundaried as possible at all times. Having a secure platform to work from means that you will be able to deal with the unexpected in the best way possible.

Chapter 4

Generic Boundaries

There are a few areas of professional boundaries that are relevant to almost all social care professions. Where the boundaries are drawn varies from sector to sector and job to job, but the principles underlying the boundaries in this chapter are fairly universal.

The overarching aim of many of these guidelines is to ensure that the relationship between worker and client is kept on a *professional* level and does not become a *personal* relationship, or appear to others to be a personal relationship. As a relationship drifts into more personal areas more and more boundary issues are likely to crop up.

It is ridiculous to think that we can remove everything of a personal nature from our interaction with clients. We are all individuals and we give out messages about who we are and what we are about on many levels all the time. However, you need to learn where to draw the line.

Given the complexity of human beings and the myriad roles and situations that social care workers find themselves in, it is not possible to provide a definitive guide of what to do in every situation. You may find that on some occasions these guidelines clash with each other, so you will have to use your professional judgement to decide which takes precedence. You should, however, retain the client's best interests at the heart of that decision. You have to use your professional judgement to decide how to apply the concepts in this chapter depending on the situation that you face.

Compassionate boundaries

This book is full of rules and guidelines for your behaviour and it is important that you follow them as closely as possible. To behave in line with the standards expected of you will take confidence – you will have to be firm and stick to your boundaries.

However, it is also important to remember that the clients who you are working with are not just statistics or caseload, they are human beings with thoughts, fears, hopes and feelings.

Your decisions and actions need to be guided by a sense of compassion for your client group (as well as for your fellow team members and for yourself). Being overly strict and authoritarian will not benefit anyone, but neither will being a 'doormat' for people to walk all over.

To get a full understanding of all the boundaries that you need to manage you should also ensure that you read Chapter 5, 'Confidentiality', Chapter 6, 'Beginnings and Endings', and Chapter 7, 'Professional Boundaries and the Law'.

How we manage boundaries

There are many different ways in which we have to manage boundaries in our work practice. The list below gives a general overview and is followed by a more detailed list of areas to consider.

We manage boundaries by:

- treating clients respectfully

- respecting and looking after ourselves and other team members

- keeping within our role

- managing interpersonal relationships

- managing our own emotions

- managing our own behaviour

- having clear and regular communication (with clients/ management/team)

- not colluding with clients

- having consistent team boundaries

- enforcing rules

- maintaining paperwork

- having boundaries for accessing service.

Confidentiality

This is the public face of professional boundaries. Almost everyone understands that social care workers provide a confidential service. If people are going to tell us a great deal of sensitive personal information they need to trust that it will be kept securely and that the worker will only divulge it when necessary. However, clients do not always understand what confidentiality really means in practice and so you should always explain your confidentiality boundaries carefully. For more information see Chapter 5, 'Confidentiality'.

Duty of care

As a social care worker you have a general duty of care to clients with whom you engage. This means that you are expected to pay attention to their well-being and address any issues that you are aware of. Addressing an issue may be as simple as talking to the client, telling another professional or making a referral. Even if the problem is well outside of your remit, if you can see that a problem exists for the client you should attempt to support the client, or get support for the client or encourage the client to get support.

Duty of care also means that you are expected to work to the best of your ability, to ensure that you have done everything that could reasonably be expected of you to look after the client. You therefore need to be diligent, focused and hard-working about your job and your clients.

Client focus

It is important that the client's needs and desires are at the centre of decisions that impact on them. If a relationship is driven by the worker's personal needs then things are entirely the wrong way round, although workers' professional needs (such as health and safety or policy and procedure) will still take precedence at times.

What is best? Who decides?

It all sounds very nice saying the client's needs come first, and most of you in most situations will have a good understanding of what you think these needs are. But who gets to decide what the client's needs are and who defines what is best for the client? What if the client and the professionals have wildly differing views on what is necessary or what is best? What if someone wants to remain in a relationship with an abusive partner for the sake of the children, or if a client does not want to accept treatment for their illness or addiction. As professionals we will hold an opinion on what we believe is best for the client, but at what point do we say that we are doing something for the client's own good despite what the client wants?

There is no easy answer to this, but it is still true that you must take into account what the client wants. For the most part you have to try to reach a consensus with your client and have a little give and take between your competing boundaries. However, there are two exceptions to this: first if the client is judged not to be 'competent' to make decisions; and second if there is a risk of significant harm to the client or others around them (see Chapter 7 for more information on safeguarding).

Client autonomy

Clients have a basic right to decide on and consent to their treatment and how to live their life. This means that clients can choose to engage in or not engage in treatment and can choose to behave in dangerous, unhealthy or unsafe ways. We can try to persuade them but we cannot force them to do things that they do not want to do. The only exception is if someone is suffering from mental health problems and they present a danger to themselves or other members of the public. They can then be forcibly taken and held in a mental health hospital or secure unit. This is an extreme measure, and for it to happen, the police, the health authority and social services all need to agree.

Transparency

Clients have a basic human right to know what is being decided or done in relation to treatment or support that involves them. It is both respectful and useful to be transparent in your actions with clients and to keep them informed at every stage of your work with them. It is very easy for clients to feel that things are happening behind closed doors and are out of their control. Ensure that you explain what you are going to do, what the implications of that are and what the outcomes might be for the client. In particular, if decisions are being made that relate to your client they have a right to know that the decisions are being made, on what grounds and by whom.

Physical contact

The basic boundary is that you should keep physical contact to a minimum and to a level appropriate to your role and your relationship. The most common issue raised by this is the giving (or not) of hugs.

Clearly, some jobs require a greater level of physical touch than others. A visit to a physiotherapist may, entirely appropriately, involve a lot of physical touch. However, a visit to a housing support worker involving a similar amount of physical contact would be deeply inappropriate.

You need to be sensitive to what is culturally normal for your clients, who may be more or less physical depending on their culture. Within most cultures, touching the hand and the lower arm is considered as fairly non-threatening and is not an overtly sexual contact and so is fairly safe. Either way, you should be very respectful of your client's personal space and aware of your own.

Physical contact can easily be misinterpreted as:

- a sign that your relationship is special or different

- a sexual advance (wanted or unwanted)

- a threatening gesture.

Hugging particularly causes issues, because hugging is something that is done by parents to children, between sexual partners or between friends. If you have a vulnerable client, a hug may spark off all sorts of feelings that are deeper than you realise.

Dealing with hugs

There are many occasions where a client will unexpectedly hug a worker, and it may be hard to shove someone away without being too aggressive or rejecting them in an unnecessarily harsh manner. If the situation occurs, the best way to deal with it is to accept the hug with the minimum of body contact and then afterwards explain that you want to keep your relationship on a professional level and that hugging is not appropriate.

A hug offered/given by a worker to a client is a more loaded gesture than a client hugging a worker unexpectedly. It implies that the worker sees the relationship as different, special or personal, or that the worker's boundaries are slack.

For a more detailed analysis of hugging see Chapter 8, 'Broken Boundaries'.

Gifts

It is very common for workers to receive gifts from clients, at Christmas time, at the end of a relationship, or as a token of thanks. This is quite normal but can be problematic. If a gift is very personal or of high value then it could distort the client–worker relationship or give the impression of some impropriety. A gift being turned down can be upsetting for the client and difficult for the worker and needs to be handled sensitively.

A gift from a worker to a client is more problematic and less usual. If a gift is given by an individual worker to a particular client and not to other clients, it would be very easy for the client or others to see the relationship between the two as 'special' or more personal.

Giving gifts is something that we normally do with friends and family and therefore automatically drags a professional relationship into a more personal arena.

Clients may expect something in return for a gift: special treatment, a return gift, the deepening of the relationship.

If a gift is of low value and not too personal it may be possible to accept it without any problems. Ideally, you will be able to accept the gift on behalf of the team/organisation/other clients, and share the gift in some way.

There are many ways that gifts from clients to workers can be handled:

- A maximum gift value that may be accepted by a workers is set.
- Workers declare any gifts that they have received to management.
- A written record of any gifts received is kept.
- Gifts can only be accepted on behalf of the team.
- Gifts are given to charity.
- Alcoholic drinks are saved and brought out at the team/ organisation Christmas party.
- There is a general ban on gifts.

However, gifts from workers to clients can only happen if it is something that happens for everyone and is depersonalised, such as at festive times, or on all clients' birthdays, they get a small gift from 'the team'.

Lending books

An issue that often crops up is the lending of books between workers and clients. On one level this can be seen as a common practice that does not have a great deal of value (we often don't expect to get a book back once we 'lend' it). However, it is still a personal interaction which singles out the relationship between the two individuals. It is also quite possible that if a book is lost or regularly forgotten then this can cause appointments to be missed or resentment/guilt to build up.

Giving out cigarettes

Another common and relatively impersonal piece of gift giving that often happens in some social care settings is giving out cigarettes. It can, however, be a double-edged sword. Sharing a cigarette is a simple way to bond and build rapport with a client, and at the right moment it is a simple ice-breaker and can calm a situation down or remove a client from a tense situation. However, there are a number of good reasons not to use this short-cut to rapport.

Smokers are automatically part of a club, and whilst it is easy to join the club you have to smoke to do so. This can make the act of giving a cigarette divisive, dividing the smoking staff members from the non-smoking staff members, the staff members who give cigarettes to clients from those who don't.

Many workers find that they can have a useful chat with clients whilst they share a cigarette break. Both the client and the worker feel more relaxed and informal in this setting, and this makes it more likely that a boundary will slip on either side. Clients may assume that this setting is different and subject to 'smoking club rules' not normal rules. Particularly if you are with a group of clients you are more likely to hear gossip, bitching or moans about the service or other workers. If you then use this information in a professional context it can be difficult for you and the clients.

It should not be forgotten that you are enabling and tacitly approving of someone's addiction – you would not offer alcohol or illegal drugs in the same way. It can be an unhealthy short-cut to building rapport, which could be replaced by the use of basic communication skills and meeting the client's needs.

The simplest solution is to have a clear policy on staff giving cigarettes to clients and have separate smoking areas for staff and clients.

Financial transactions

With the exception of standard pre-arranged payments for services that would be paid by any other client, and payments that come from an organisation to a client that are handled by workers, no money should be exchanged between clients and workers at all. Giving, lending or borrowing money is something that family and friends would normally do and therefore drags the relationship into a more personal arena.

It is not appropriate to give, receive, lend or borrow money from clients in any way. It can:

• make it appear that a relationship is inappropriate

- leave the client with expectations of receiving more money
- generate resentment/guilt/ill feeling between worker and client
- build dependence on the worker or on the funds
- leave the worker or client vulnerable to abuse.

Personal details

Do not give your personal address or phone number to your clients. The act of you giving the details to them automatically makes the relationship more personal and contains an implicit invitation to the client to phone or visit you. If a client starts phoning you or visiting you outside of work hours it is very easy for many other boundaries to fall. It is important that you have time off outside of work to recharge your batteries and relax. There are also obvious health and safety concerns.

It is possible that clients may learn where you live, especially if you live in the area that you work in. This is not an ideal situation, but is not as problematic as you giving them your details.

Self-disclosure

Difficulties arise with this boundary because most human relationships are built by sharing experiences and information about yourself with others. When humans relate to each other and build relationships (or rapport) we often exchange information, and we all like to know details of the lives of those around us. As a worker you often know a great deal about your clients, and it is natural human interest that they will want to know about you.

However, you should disclose as little as possible about your personal life to clients. The greater the emotional or therapeutic your relationship, the more important this rule is. The more in-depth and personal the information, the more likely it is to cause boundary issues.

In its strictest form this rule comes from psychotherapy, and some psychotherapists practise it to an extreme level. Most social care workers can and should be slightly more relaxed than a psychotherapist in relation to self-disclosure, but it is still something you should be very careful about.

Unless you work in very controlled surroundings or exhibit remarkable focus on anonymity it is very hard to keep all personal details about yourself from the client. Clients will see if you have a wedding ring, they may notice you wearing a football shirt, or see a sticker on your car, overhear conversations or see photos on your desk.

These things are to a certain extent unavoidable and for the most part you don't need to worry about them. First, they are the kind of details that are common knowledge, not very in-depth or very personal. There is also an important difference between someone finding out a piece of information about you, and you telling them that piece of information. If you voluntarily share some information about yourself with a client, it contains an implicit message that this is a personal relationship. You and your client may not be consciously aware, but it will shift the axis of your relationship. The question that you have to ask yourself is, why are you telling your client this piece of information, what is the purpose and whose needs does it serve?

There are a number of possible problems that can be caused by disclosing too much information, including:

- *Transference.* The more a client knows about you, the more likely they are to confuse their relationship with you with other significant relationships in their life. (For more information see Chapter 9, 'Understanding Negative Consequences'.)

- *Shift of focus.* The focus of your relationship with your clients should be them. The more you bring your own life into the relationship, the less clear this becomes. Your emotions and your needs can start to impinge on the focus of the relationship.

- *Encouraging clients to see you as a friend.* The more your clients know about you, the more personal your relationship becomes and the more likely it is that they will become confused about your role.

- *Creating dependency.* The more information you and your client share, the greater the personal bond between you and the more likely the client is to become dependent upon you.

Sharing information about your personal issues/background

It is very common for people to work in a particular field if they have had some experience of the issues that are dealt with in that field (either personally or through family members). For example, people who were homeless may work in the housing field; people who have suffered from addiction may work in the substance misuse field.

Particularly in the addictions field, clients will quickly make a judgement about whether you have, or have not, had an addiction and will often challenge you about it.

It is also very easy when someone is working through a particular issue that you have suffered from to give and share examples of how it was for you and how you dealt with it. It is particularly easy to fall into this habit if the issue is new and confusing for the client.

Disclosing information about the issues or circumstances of your life can be a very powerful tool and can build a great deal of rapport and trust with clients, it can also give clients hope that they can move on from their issues. However, it is a double-edged sword and should be dealt with very carefully.

Not only are you sharing an in-depth and personal piece of information about yourself, but it is a piece of information which will have a natural bonding effect between you which makes the relationship more personal and more special.

It can also have the effect of splitting teams, if the clients know that some workers have been through a personal experience and some have not. Clients can act as if the workers with the experience are the only ones that can help them, or know what they are talking about.

The question you need to ask yourself is, does the knowledge that you have experienced certain issues help this client in their recovery/progress? It is better to demonstrate the in-depth knowledge and understanding your experience gives you through your actions and the way that you relate to people and understand their issues.

The converse of this issue is that letting clients know that you have not been through a particular life experience is also revealing something of yourself. It is not as personal as revealing what you have done, but it can nonetheless create some problems.

Twelve-step programmes/self-help groups

It is not uncommon for workers to still be receiving help from support groups, in particular 12-step recovery programmes, whilst working in a related social care project. There is therefore a reasonable chance that you could attend the same meeting or group as one of your clients.

This may cause some discomfort for both worker and client in terms of what is disclosed in the group/meeting. Either the worker or the client may feel inhibited about accessing the group or sharing certain information. However, both the worker and the client have a right to access and make use of the full support that is available to them.

All of these support groups have strict rules of confidentiality and in theory these will avoid many possible problems as long as everyone keeps to them. However, it takes a lot of trust on both sides, particularly as the groups are open access and anyone can attend at any stage of their recovery/process.

There may also be issues for the worker with a clash of professional boundaries and group boundaries. For example, if the worker discovers that a client is breaking rules of the project, or lying to staff. On a personal level it would be ethical for the worker to keep the confidentiality of the group. But this could cause a clash with a variety of professional boundaries.

Depending on the nature of the issue, it is up to the individual to decide how to deal with the situation. However, the worker should speak to their manager about the situation as soon as it arises, have a chat to the client to establish boundaries and should, if possible, make an effort to attend a different meeting or group.

Dual relationships

In order to keep your relationship with your clients straightforward, unambiguous and unclouded by any other issues you should ensure that you have only one relationship with a client.

You should ensure that you do not hold any of the following relationships with a client whilst you are a worker for a service that they are engaging with: family member, friend, sexual partner, employee, employer, customer/client. This applies before, during and after your working relationship.

It may be that your client is a stockbroker and could advise you on your share investments, or offer carpentry services that would save you money. Having more than one role will produce a variety of conflicts that will start to break other boundaries.

This boundary is particularly hard to maintain if you live and work within small or isolated communities. There may have to be some give in the boundary if, for example, you are the only mental health worker and your client is the only doctor in an isolated area.

Sexual relationships

Very clearly it is totally unacceptable for a worker to engage in a sexual relationship or sexual behaviour with a client or an ex-client. It is abusive, inappropriate, a misuse of power and sends out entirely the wrong message. There is no good excuse or reason for any kind of sexual contact with your clients. It should be noted that sexual behaviour extends to flirting or flirtatious behaviour, sexual jokes or innuendo and discussions about sexual issues that are not relevant to your role. It is very common for a client to form a romantic attachment to their worker and you must be very careful not to encourage this.

Personal relationships

Be very clear: you are not, and should not be, your client's friend. You may meet some lovely people, with whom you would become firm friends in another setting. But friends do all sorts of things that clients and workers don't do: bend the rules, keep secrets, lend money, socialise, do favours and all sorts of other unprofessional behaviour. You should not form a social relationship with a current or ex-client outside of work hours. This means that you should not just meet for a coffee, call them or do anything to initiate any kind of personal relationship. If they need to see you, it should be done in work hours within a work setting.

When does a client stop being a client?

Rules about the nature of your relationship with clients (such as the rules about sexual, personal, financial or dual relationships) could be seen to label individuals as clients indefinitely. People often ask if these rules are permanent. It is unfair for individuals to be labelled for life because they needed support around a particular issue at one point in their lives.

This is an area of some debate. In most cases, if a client stops being a client, not just for you, but also the organisation that you work for, and you do not have any kind of relationship or contact for at least two years, if you meet again it would seem reasonable that you are entitled to start fresh.

You should nonetheless be careful about entering into a personal or sexual relationship that has its roots as worker and client, particularly if the relationship was deep and therapeutic (e.g. counselling or psychotherapy). This may sometimes be difficult, for example if your project employs ex-clients or uses them as volunteers or if you live and work in a small community.

Special relationships

It is important that we treat clients fairly and consistently, that we don't bend the rules for or favour the clients that we like, or come down extra hard on the clients that we don't like. This is first because it is fair and ethical to do so and because we need to respect people's differences, but also because if clients feel that someone is getting special treatment then it can build a lot of resentment which is counter-productive for all concerned.

It is natural to have clients whom we like more than others, and for that matter clients we dislike, or who wind us up. However, it is important that you put these feelings to one side as much as possible. Other clients and staff members will pick up very quickly if someone gets special treatment or is treated unfairly.

This may be a challenge if you get on very well with a client or identify with them, or on the other hand if they are insolent, rude or they act in ways that you find repugnant.

Professionalism and boundaries

As well as considering the relationship you have with your client, there are a host of professional requirements that you also need to fulfil.

Safeguarding

You must watch out for, record and report any signs of abuse happening to children or vulnerable adults. (See Chapter 7, 'Professional Boundaries and the Law', for more details.) This means that you need to understand the different categories of abuse and know what signs to look out for. Ensure that you receive sufficient training in this area.

Discrimination

We all have a duty to ensure that our services, the way they are provided and publicised, do not discriminate against any particular groups. Many of the boundaries mentioned in this chapter are focused on preventing discrimination.

It is important as part of anti-discriminatory practice to treat every client as an individual and not to make assumptions about them. Make sure that you check yourself for any assumptions you make about clients, and ensure that you do a full assessment of clients' needs and check out anything you are unsure about with them.

It also means that as a worker you need to leave your personal prejudices at home. As a social care worker you are obliged to provide an equal service to all clients. Most of us are aware of the standard groups that we should not discriminate against, but how would you feel providing a service to a convicted paedophile, or a rapist? We all have personal views and experiences that will colour our perception of certain groups, but they all have a right to a service. (See Chapter 7, 'Professional Boundaries and the Law', for more details.)

Maintenance of rules/boundaries

It might seem unnecessary to say in a book about boundaries, but it is very important that workers enforce rules and boundaries consistently and fairly at all times. If you don't you will be undermining your ability, and the ability of your team, to manage boundaries. If you bend a rule one week and another worker tries to enforce it the following week, they are more likely to get a problematic response from clients as a result. If clients and staff know that they can get different answers from different members of staff, then clients can exploit this to create divisions in the team or manipulate staff members. If you fail to maintain some boundaries you are increasing the chance of others being crossed.

Health and safety

Health and safety has had a bad press in recent times, but ultimately the health and safety of yourself, your clients and fellow workers is very much your concern and your duty.

There is not space in this book to cover all aspects of health and safety, and much health and safety will relate to your particular workplace. However, you should ensure that you understand all health and safety policies for your workplace, and ensure that you follow them. They will be there to protect you and your clients. Policies which are commonly ignored, and should not be, are: lone working, carrying of personal alarms and risk assessment.

Personal safety

Your safety is a key boundary that should not be ignored. Social care is about meeting other people's needs, but that does not mean that your needs are swept under the carpet. It is important that you do not place yourself in physical or emotional danger. Most organisations will have a number of policies in place to ensure your safety, and of course you should follow those. Outside of these policies you need to make a judgement about your personal safety and if you are not comfortable about it then you should leave the situation, get some support from fellow staff members or take whatever action is needed to protect yourself.

Policy and procedure

Every job/organisation will have its own set of policies and procedures. It is vital that you act in line with these, unless you have specific permission not to do so. Whilst they can never provide a guide to every action, they are your common guideline to ensure consistency amongst your team. They will have been thought about and based on past experience and may sometimes be there to deal with a situation that you have not come across before.

They are also your protection and support system. If you work and abide by the policies and procedures of your workplace then your employer should support you if anything goes wrong. If you decide to work off-plan and to do things your own way, then you are by default taking responsibility yourself. If you are faced with a serious incident or client death or injury this can be a very serious matter.

Boundaries for access to service

Most organisations will have criteria for who they will or won't (can or can't) accept in their service. It may be defined by level of support need, or for people who suffer from particular issues, or maybe a particular client group. These boundaries are very, very important and should never be ignored (although it is common for both workers on the ground and management to overrule these policies). A service will have been designed with particular clients in mind; staff will have been recruited with the right skill set and in the right numbers to deal with these clients. Once you accept a client into your service you are honour-bound to work with them if at all possible (assuming they have been honest in their assessment/referral information). Trying to support an unsuitable client within your service will certainly lead to other boundaries being broken and is unfair to the client in question and other clients in the project.

Teamwork

If you do work with a team of fellow professionals it is important that you work closely together and support each other, particularly around boundary issues.

You should try as much as possible to keep your enforcement of boundaries in line with each other so that there is a consistent approach. There will always be some disparity and it is common to have an 'enforcer' on the team who restores order and enforces rules, and a 'soft touch' who will let clients get away with crossing boundaries. This set-up leads to divisions within the team and resentments amongst both staff and clients.

You also need to support and back up your fellow team members in front of clients wherever possible to show unity amongst the team. This does not mean that you have to mindlessly support everything that your team members do. But you should not criticise them in front of clients and if a client brings up some inappropriate behaviour, get information from them and promise that you will ensure that the matter is dealt with properly.

Working within your role/competence

We all have limits to our skills and experience and it is important to recognise when we have reached these limits. Some clients will need to be supported by professionals with other specialisms or other roles and remits. As a responsible worker you need to know when it is time to make a referral. Not only should you not try to support a client if you do not have the necessary experience/qualifications, but it is also important that you maintain the focus of your role and work on the task that is part of your role.

If you have a particularly tricky client you may need to refer them to someone within the same field but with more experience. If you are a drugs worker and your client shows signs of mental health problems you should refer them to a mental health specialist service or worker, even if you have experience of mental health issues. If you are a home care worker and your client has emotional issues that need dealing with you should refer them to a counsellor.

It is easy to get caught up with a client who you like, and who you work with well, and think you can do everything for them. If you find yourself feeling reluctant to hand over a client to other professionals, then you have become overly attached to the client.

Use of language

Most social care professionals rely on their communication skills to do their job well. To ensure our message gets across clearly we need to use clear and appropriate language when speaking to clients. As the professional, it is your duty to ensure that you communicate in language that is at an appropriate level for the clients to understand and do not use language that will alienate, upset or impact on them too greatly. Vulnerable clients can become easily confused, may be sensitive, and may pick up what you say to them and the words that you use. You should always use language that is unambiguous and clear in its meaning. If something could be taken to mean something else, or understood in a different way from how you meant it, it can lead to confusion and problems.

It should go without saying that you must not use language that could be offensive to any particular group (e.g. racist, sexist, ageist language). You should also avoid swearing and other offensive language.

TERMINOLOGY

The social care sector is full of initials, shortenings, technical terms and language that enables professionals to talk about clients and issues quickly and easily. It would be very easy to baffle and confuse them with terminology, initials and complex language. Wherever possible, use language that is simple and easy to understand. As you get to know a client you will be able to judge their level of understanding and vocabulary and change the language you use appropriately. If you are talking about a complex subject, or using technical terms (which are sometime unavoidable), ensure that you check your client's understanding of what you are saying.

LABELLING

If someone gets told something about themselves often enough they will start to internalise and take on board the information in how they view themselves. If someone has low self-esteem then this process is heightened and amplified. As professionals we need to be careful that the language we use to describe clients does not become one of these internalised labels. We are seen as the 'experts' and so clients can take what we say very seriously. If, for example, we very frequently describe a client as 'dependent' or 'vulnerable', this can become part of the client's internal script and become a self-fulfilling prophesy.

COMPLIMENTS

Often it is part of a worker's job to help build a client's confidence, and complimenting a client is a natural and useful part of that work. However, you need to be very careful that your compliments are unambiguous and could not be misinterpreted as flirting, a sexual advance or as an indication of a more personal relationship between you. Make sure that your compliments are accurate, appropriate and not too personal.

For example, there is a clear difference between 'You're looking good today' and 'You look very smart today'. 'Smart' is a much more objective word and has an obvious meaning. 'Good' could mean 'good looking' or 'smart' and could be taken very differently by the client.

Words such as 'special' which do not have a clear meaning (e.g. 'special needs', 'special relationship', 'my special…', 'special case') should also be avoided, as they can have many connotations.

SLANG

At times the use of slang can be very useful to establish rapport with a particular client or client group and to show that you understand them or their issues on a certain level. However, be very careful when using slang. If you use it incorrectly, or use out-of-date, old-fashioned slang, then it will undermine you; there is also the danger that the client may not know the slang but may not want to look unknowledgeable by asking you what it means.

NICKNAMES

It is not unusual for people to have or to use nicknames for other people. For the most part you should not use or accept them as a worker. If a nickname is personal between two people and only they use it, it is a bond and a sign of intimacy and therefore takes the relationship into personal territory. Nicknames often create a feeling of cliquishness which is also unhelpful.

Many nicknames reinforce stereotypes of perceptions of an individual, both for the individual with the nickname and by others, particularly if it is a long-standing nickname.

Collusion with clients

There are many situations when it is the professional's responsibility to maintain their objectivity and professional stance in the face of the client's behaviour. It can be very easy to get swept up into agreeing with a client, not challenging a client or accepting certain behaviour from a client. It is important that you do not condone inappropriate behaviour from a client or even be seen by the client to be condoning the behaviour by not challenging it.

If a client is lying, bending the rules, or doing something illegal, at the very least you need to point out the negative aspects of what they are doing. You should not get into an argument with the client, or become judgemental about what they are doing, but neither should it appear that you think it is acceptable.

Sometimes a client will avoid talking about a particular subject, will be in denial about something. You have to make a professional judgement about when and how to approach the subject, but make sure that you are not mirroring their behaviour and helping them avoid it.

Other clients may have incorrect beliefs, fantasies or mistaken ideas about themselves, other people or situations. Wherever possible you should point out to them their error and provide a more balanced realistic assessment of the situation.

Colluding with staff

Do not collude with other staff who are breaking boundaries – you are just enabling and protecting them. If you are unable to talk to the member of staff in question then you should take it to your manager. If you are aware that a member of staff is breaking boundaries and do nothing about it you have a certain level of responsibility for the consequences of those actions. Our role is to protect and support our clients and this should be our number one priority. If the needs of fellow staff members come before those of clients then problems will start to build up.

Looking after yourself

Keeping clients' needs at the centre of your work is clearly important, as is making sure that you respect their rights, boundaries and autonomy. However, workers have needs too and these should not be ignored. You have a responsibility to ensure that you are fit to work and that you attend to your needs as a professional.

If you never took breaks, ignored personal safety, worked an extra five hours a day, worked when you were sick and never took time off for meetings, training and line management, you would soon become burnt out and your work practice and personal life would suffer. You would soon become of less and less use to your clients and other boundaries would start to slip.

However, if you took time off whenever you felt a bit tired, cut short client meetings so you could go shopping and answered personal phone calls during meetings you would be meeting your needs ahead of the clients'.

The important difference is between your professional needs and responsibilities and your personal needs. Your professional needs can be put in front of client needs in some situations, but there is of course a balance – and don't forget your responsibility to yourself.

Professional needs

Time off
You have the right to time off for relaxation/holidays and time off if you are ill.

Training
You should expect to be either employed for work that you trained for, or trained to do tasks for which you are not qualified.

Realistic workload
You should have a workload that is achievable within your working hours. It should be possible to meet your clients' needs adequately within these hours.

Support/management

You should have access to suitable support systems and have an effective system of management in place to meet your needs.

Suitable resources and working environment

The environment you work in should be safe, secure and suitable for the work that you do.

Personal safety

You should not be placed at unnecessary physical or mental risk as a result of work practices or structure.

Unfortunately many social care workers are in a very pressurised environment without enough staff or resources to get their professional needs met. High caseloads, little or no training, inadequate management and unsuitable premises are all worryingly common in the sector, both in publicly funded and private institutions. Sometimes you may have to be realistic and accept a less than perfect working environment. However, the truth is that organisations have a responsibility to their workers and their clients to provide certain minimum standards. If these standards are not being met then these organisations are being professionally negligent.

If you believe that your professional needs are not being met to such an extent that you or the clients you work with are in danger, then you need to make sure that you raise the issue with your manager. For further information see the section on 'Whistleblowing' below.

Dealing with complaints

Accepting complaints from clients and dealing with them appropriately is another key part of a professional service. Any complaints need to be taken seriously until proved otherwise. We don't like to believe anything bad of our colleagues, but you have to be open to the possibility that they have done something wrong. It is important that clients feel able to make complaints and that they will be taken seriously. Many abuses go undetected because the victims do not feel able to complain.

If a client does make a complaint about a fellow worker or a professional from another service then you should take notes as soon as possible, recording their words as accurately as possible, not ask any leading questions or put words into their mouth and tell them that this will be taken seriously, investigated and dealt with appropriately.

If the matter is very minor then you can approach the worker and discuss what has happened. However, if it is a matter that could be seen as abuse or as misconduct then you need to talk to your manager, or someone in a position of seniority over the worker.

Managing workload

It is important that you manage your workload so that you are able to give clients sufficient attention, complete relevant paperwork and do any other administrative tasks. If you take on a workload that is too high then all of your clients will suffer as your time is squeezed.

If you are lucky enough to have control over how many clients you take onto your caseload (either because you are in private practice or you have sufficient power within your organisation) then you should be able to manage this reasonably easily.

However, many workers, particularly in the statutory sector, do not have a choice over the size of their caseload. If you are in a position where you feel that your workload is unmanageable, either because you are becoming stressed or burnt out, then you need to speak to your line manager/supervisor immediately. If your manager does not know that you are overworked and you just keep accepting clients they will keep sending them to you.

First, you need to look at your work practice and ensure that you are working efficiently and effectively enough and see if you could streamline any processes. If there are no improvements that can be made then your caseload is too high to be effectively managed. If you work in private practice then you need to cut down your caseload over time as clients leave.

If your manager/organisation insists that you carry a caseload that is too high, then there are insufficient workers/resources to meet the needs of the clients. This places the pressure on the workers and the consequences will be that outcomes for clients will suffer. If, as an individual, or as a team, you accept the excessive workload, you are effectively colluding with your organisation in providing a second-rate service. If the workload is leading to seriously dangerous practice then you should consider whistleblowing (see below).

The reality for many workers is that their workload is stressful and only by careful (or frantic) juggling can they manage the work. It is fair for organisations to expect some hard work and some flexibility from their workers, and the practicalities of earning a wage and the reality of funding levels may make this area an unavoidable boundary crossing for some people.

Whistleblowing

If you feel that the working practices in your place of work are negligent, dangerous, abusive, dishonest or in any other way unsuitable then you have a duty to try your best to alert more senior people in the organisation so that things can change. Your first port of call would be your line manager, then, if no action is taken or you are ignored, you should raise the issue with their line manager. If need be you should take your complaint to the top of the organisation. (Many social care organisations will have a board of governors which can be appealed to above and beyond the managing director.)

If you have complained internally and no action is being taken then you have the right to tell someone outside of the organisation (this is known as 'whistleblowing'). Not only do you have a duty to do this in serious cases, but you also have the right to do so without being discriminated against in your employment with the organisation. However, do remember that you only have this right if you have made every effort to deal with the issues internally and that when you raise the issue externally it is with the correct authority and with the aim of improving the situation.

If you have a situation where you think whistleblowing is necessary then you should contact the funders of the organisation, the professional body or the government department responsible rather than going straight to the press. If you still get no action from the relevant responsible bodies you do then have the right to go to the press.

Maintaining an appropriate relationship

There are many ways in a which a relationship between a client and worker can be inappropriate or off track. Most of them revolve around a relationship becoming too personal. As a worker it is your responsibility to watch out for signs that the relationship is heading off track and to take action to ensure that it stays on track.

Setting an example

To a greater or lesser extent, workers will act as role models for their clients. You will find that often clients will mirror the behaviour and attitudes of their worker. You therefore need to act in an appropriate manner. If you have a lack of boundaries, your clients will have fewer boundaries. If you are often angry, your clients will be more angry. Therefore you should be positive, realistic, independent, responsible, thoughtful, polite and/or any other qualities desirable in your clients.

Empowering clients

This is a general aim of most social care services and there are many things that you can do to assist. In the context of boundaries it is about making sure that you do not disempower the clients by doing everything for them. This can occur on both practical and emotional levels.

On a practical level, if clients are feeling low in energy, lacking in confidence about their abilities and unmotivated then they may naturally want you to do things for them – make that phone call, fill in a form, go with them to appointments. There are times when doing these things is a useful service that you can provide for clients, but you must be aware that your job is to get closer to the stage where they can do these things for themselves. If they never practise these things, or learn the skills, they will forever be dependent on you.

> Proverb: 'Give a man a fish and you feed him for a day. Teach a man to fish and you feed him for a lifetime.'

On an emotional level you can do the work for people by using your energy to cheer them up, make them feel better or make decisions for them. If you do spend your time and energy propping up their moods and feelings, not only will you become tired and drained but their happiness will depend on having you around. This will lead to an emotional dependency which is not healthy for either of you. (See Chapter 9, 'Understanding Negative Consequences', for more details.)

Objectivity

None of us can be truly objective, but we should try as much as possible to maintain an unbiased and balanced viewpoint of our clients at all times. Wherever possible we should try to keep our professional opinion untainted by our personal experience and opinions. This enables us to have a professional overview of a client's situation and to keep our minds open.

It is very easy to superimpose your experience, your solutions or your past history or your opinions onto what you know of the client. This narrows your focus of your thinking, leads to assumptions and can cloud your judgement.

You will have, and will continue to develop, a professional opinion about your area of work. This will involve making some subjective judgements. When working with people, emotions and feelings, there may not be solid facts and we sometimes have to work with our intuition and our feelings. However, it is still important that you run a little self-check on yourself to ensure that your judgements are as objective as possible.

Objective vs. subjective

Overall, the difference between objective and subjective information is the difference between fact and opinion:

Objective	Subjective
Can be observed	Formed by opinion
Can be described	Based on personal judgement
Can be counted or quantified	Based on a belief
Close to 'the truth'	Varies from person to person
Factual	Based on myth or rumour

If you have something that is not objective and that may have many possible answers, none of which are clearly 'the truth', you can still deal with this in an objective manner. If you present a balanced and unbiased report on the various options this can be considered to be objective.

Unconditional positive regard

Being non-judgemental is a very simple cornerstone of social care work. It is important that we accept our clients and the issues that they bring to us without criticising them. In practice this means that you need to be accepting and non-judgemental of who they are and what they tell you.

This is a concept that grew from humanistic counselling and was introduced by Carl Rogers in his 1961 book, *On Becoming a Person*. This book was about and aimed at one-to-one counsellors but many of the concepts have become embedded in the way most social care professionals work.

No one likes to be judged, and most of our clients will get enough judgement from society or other people in their life. We want them to be free to engage and share information with us; if they are worried about what we will think or how we will react then they will share much less.

The position of power that we have in relation to our clients means that they will internalise and take on board what we say and how we react. To grow and change as people we all need to feel good about ourselves. If we are disapproving, negative and judgemental about them, it will very quickly lower their self-esteem. It can be very tough to remain non-judgemental in the face of aggressive, negative or self-defeating behaviour or when our clients act in ways that we disapprove of or find difficult to accept.

Offloading

If you are stressed out, in a bad mood or feeling low and someone asks you how you are, it is very easy to really let rip and offload your feelings. Whilst it is acceptable to acknowledge that you are not feeling at your best, or you are a bit tired, you should not dump your feelings onto the client and bring your personal life or feelings into the relationship.

It is particularly important that you do not bring any negative feelings about your team, your service or your manager to the clients. If you have grievances you should air them in the proper forums. Your negativity will give the implicit go-ahead to the client to be negative and will highlight splits in the team. However, you don't need to be relentlessly positive, and you can acknowledge negatives that they bring up if they are realistic and reasonable.

Timekeeping

It is important that you ensure that there are some time boundaries for the work that you do for clients, whatever role you are in. You should regulate the length of time that you spend with a client and manage timekeeping for both you and your client.

It is important to retain some flexibility to meet the needs of particularly chaotic clients. However, you should expect most clients to be able to manage their own time so that you are able to manage your own time. Allowing them to turn up late, cancel sessions or not to turn up whenever they feel like it will feed into their lack of motivation or disorganisation. It will also give the impression that your time is not valuable and the sessions are not important or worth bothering with.

Structure

If possible you should have fixed arrangements about when you see the clients and/or how long you spend with a particular client. Giving clients some structure to when they see you provides a sense of regularity and security that will help them engage with you. If you are chaotic about when you see them, you can expect to get a more chaotic response from them. If you are engaged in a therapeutic relationship with your clients, then having some fixed elements in the relationship provides a stable 'frame' for them to explore issues which may make them feel unstable or chaotic.

Time management

For both your sake and the sake of your clients, it is important that you manage the amount of time that you spend with them. You should decide in advance a suitable amount of time to spend with a particular client or group of clients and unless there are very pressing reasons you should stick to that allocated time.

If your group is supposed to finish at three o'clock, then you should finish on time. If your one-to-one session is supposed to be for an hour then it should last an hour. If you are supposed to do three hours of home care for a client then you should only do three hours. Running over time demonstrates poor boundaries to the client, means that some other area of your work (possibly some other clients) will suffer and will lead to you becoming more stressed and overworked.

It is important for clients to understand when a session is going to finish in order to help them understand when to start the process of winding the session down and re-setting their own emotional boundaries. Clients can feel raw and vulnerable after opening up to a worker and they should end the session with an appropriate sense of ending. You should help with the process by warning clients as a session approaches its end.

Time/place

It is simple, but important, to ensure that you are meeting with clients at an appropriate time and place. Depending on the role and on the client, what is appropriate can vary. But be aware that the situations that you meet and find yourself in change how you and your client act or perceive each other.

It is not entirely inappropriate in some situations to meet with a client in a café on a working afternoon. However, you should be aware that this is more likely to lead to off-topic chit-chat and lend a personal tone to the meeting. It is also not a confidential environment. Meeting in that same café at seven o'clock on a Saturday night would feel even more like a social occasion (or even a date).

You also need to be aware that boundaries change depending on the time and the place. If you are doing street outreach work then your health and safety boundaries will be much tighter than if you were working with your team in your office. If you are working in someone's home, you are in their territory, but it is also your place of work and they need to have some respect for that fact too.

Completing paperwork

This is a very basic, quite simple boundary that has implications for many other boundaries. The lack of information on a form or file can lead to huge problems. If you are off sick, or even just at a meeting, crucial decisions may need to be made based on your notes and forms. If all the relevant information is not recorded then the wrong decision can be made or something may not be put in place that ought to be.

If a serious issue such as the death of a client or a serious safeguarding issue arises, then your notes and files may be taken, sealed and gone through in detail to see if you have done your job properly. If the work you have done is not recorded in your notes, it may look very bad for you or the organisation that you work for.

Professional development

As a responsible professional you need to take responsibility for your own development and training. It is important that you are properly qualified and/or knowledgeable about your area of work. Whether it is changes in legislation, local services or new ways of working, you should be on top of it. If you work for an organisation they also have a responsibility, but if they don't provide you with the training/support that you need you still have an obligation to ensure that your skills and knowledge are adequate.

Even if you have received good training and are well experienced, you should continue to train and develop yourself. There is the ever-present danger that you can become stagnant or sloppy in your work practice and your knowledge can become out of date.

Politics and religion

In the social care sector there are many people with many different views, opinions, political beliefs and religious views. You can believe whatever you wish in your personal life. However, whilst working with clients it is important that you do not try to impose your views or try to persuade clients of your viewpoint. Unless is a necessary professional context, it is best to avoid getting into a discussion about religion or politics with clients. Not only will you soon slip into the realm of self-disclosure, but your viewpoint could be very alienating to certain clients.

Behaviour outside work

Unfortunately, as a social care professional you do have certain responsibilities that start to impinge on your life outside work. You have a responsibility not to bring your organisation into disrepute. This is of course true of most professionals, but because of the sensitive nature of the work that care workers do and the issues that your clients face, you have a slightly greater responsibility. If, for example, someone who worked in a bank was seen reeling drunkenly down the road, people may not think much of it. However, if a social worker did the same thing, particularly somewhere they were likely to bump into their clients, it would be seen in a different light. If a substance misuse worker gets arrested for taking drugs, or is seen taking them, then this would of course be a bigger issue than for a sales assistant.

If you are in a situation where you might bump into clients or where you can easily be identified as a member of staff at a particular organisation (e.g. on a works night out), then you need to maintain a higher standard of behaviour than you would normally.

Chapter 5

Confidentiality

Confidentiality is a cornerstone of almost all social and medical care and will be a part of your job whatever your role. It is one of the most important professional boundaries and one that you need to keep an eye on constantly. You will have access to all sorts of information about a client that you are obliged to keep confidential. It is important that clients are able to trust you with information about themselves, whether it is their medical history, sensitive information that they divulge to you or their personal history. There are both legal and ethical reasons for keeping information confidential.

However, keeping information confidential is not the same as keeping it secret. There are circumstances where you will share information as a matter of course with your line manager or team members and situations where you will be obliged to break confidentiality. It is very important that you explain this very clearly to clients in advance. They need to understand the difference between confidentiality and secrecy, what level of confidentiality they can expect from you and when you might break confidentiality. If clients understand the consequences of divulging certain information they can then make an informed decision about telling you. This ensures that the process of sharing information is fair, transparent and open.

Confidentiality and the law

Below is a summary of UK law as it relates to confidentiality. However, it is only a summary, so if you are responsible for storing information or taking information yourself you should do further research.

In many countries outside of the UK, particularly the United States, Canada, Australia, New Zealand and the rest of Europe, you will find that the legislation and practice is broadly similar. However, there are regional differences and your responsibility is to research the local law and its implications. The relevant professional bodies in your country should be able to advise you (see Appendix I, 'Useful Organisations').

The Data Protection Act 1998

This Act deals with how you store, handle and manage information provided to you by clients or customers. It covers any business, organisation or individual who takes information from members of the public. It places an obligation on you to take measures to secure information which you store or transmit, to disclose what you will use information for, and to allow individuals access to any information that is stored about them. The Data Protection Act does allow you to release information relating to the detection and prevention of crime if requested.

Safeguarding Vulnerable Groups Act 2006 and Protection of Vulnerable Groups (Scotland) Act 2007

These Acts were brought in to consolidate guidance and legislation relating to children and vulnerable adults. The Acts specify that you must disclose information relating to the abuse of vulnerable adults or children to the appropriate authorities.

Terrorism Act 2000

This Act places an obligation on all professionals and members of the public to disclose any information they have relating to acts or potential acts of terrorism.

Serious Crime Act 2007

This Act allows certain data relating to the detection of fraud to be disclosed and used for data matching.

Misuse of Drugs Act 1971

This Act has particular relevance for social care organisations that have clients on their premises. It says that if you allow drugs to be used or sold on your premises then you can be prosecuted. It was given particular relevance when two hostel managers from Cambridge were prosecuted in 1999 and given four and five year prison sentences. They allegedly knew about the drug dealing and did not do enough to prevent it and did not inform the police.

Freedom of Information Act 2000 and Freedom of Information (Scotland) Act 2002

Whilst most of these Acts is about the duty of public bodies to disclose information, they do provide an exemption for 'personal data' and therefore freedom of information requests do not impinge on clients' personal information.

Common law

There are many laws and previous rulings relating to confidentiality in the UK, all adding up to what is called 'Common Law' (see Appendix II, 'Further Reading'). The common law on confidentiality adds up to the fact that you can only disclose confidential information under three circumstances:

- The individual to whom the information relates has given consent.

- There is a legal duty to do so.

- The disclosure of the information is in the public interest.

The first two are simple enough to understand, but more tricky is to decide what is in the public interest. For the most part the public interest is the prevention of harm to self and others.

Confidentiality policies

As a member of staff your organisation should have adequate policies and procedures in place to cover all confidentiality requirements. You must ensure that you follow organisational policy and procedures on data handling and confidentiality, for your own good, the good of the organisation and the good of the clients.

A fairly standard confidentiality policy would contain something like this:

Carers R Us will keep all client information confidential and will not share that information with other individuals or organisations without the client's express permission or unless deemed necessary according to law and best practice.

Information provided to Carers R Us may be shared with other Carers R Us staff members. Information will be shared as necessary for your care.

This confidentiality may be breached under the following circumstances:

- *The information received relates to harm, or suspected harm, to a child.*

- *The information received relates to harm, or suspected harm, to yourself or others.*

- *The information received relates to abuse of, or harm to, a vulnerable adult.*

- *A court, or court order, demands that we do so.*

- *The information relates to actual or pending serious criminal activity.*

- *The information relates to the sale of illegal drugs on Carers R Us property.*

- *The information relates to acts of terrorism.*

Clients have the right, at any time, with prior notice, to see any information which is stored by Carers R Us or written about them by members of staff.

The information that Carers R Us takes will be used solely to inform and support the care provided to you by Carers R Us and will not be shared with any commercial organisations for marketing purposes.

Some de-personalised information may be shared with funders or government bodies for monitoring and research purposes. This information will not be used to identify individuals.

This example covers most of the key areas of legislation. It is your professional responsibility to understand your own organisation's confidentiality policy. If you work in particular settings with particular client groups the level of confidentiality may change. Make sure that you have studied the confidentiality policy of your organisation and that you explain it to clients in advance.

Confidentiality in action

Worker: Jane, a mental health worker

Client: Sue, a mother of two who is suffering from undiagnosed depression

Setting: A drop-in mental health clinic in a community centre

Sue has finally built up the confidence to speak to someone. She is finding it very hard to get out of bed and her two young children are being neglected as a result. She is nervous about telling anyone about her problems and it has taken a lot of courage to come down to the community centre.

Scenario 1

Jane tells her that she offers a confidential service and asks Sue to tell her a little about her situation. Sue explains everything in great detail. Jane explains the support she can offer and they book another appointment to discuss the situation further. Jane has concerns about the neglect of Sue's children and so contacts social services. Social services have had previous reports of concern about Sue and they get in touch with her to discuss providing some support for her.

Sue is surprised and scared that social services have got in touch and thinks her kids will be taken away. She feels betrayed by Jane and refuses to engage with her, puts the phone down on social services and stops answering her door. Social services become concerned and escalate the case. Sue eventually engages with social services but her trust in the local mental health service is broken.

Scenario 2

Jane explains that she offers a confidential service, but that if she has any information relating to harm or neglect to children she may have to disclose information to social services. Initially Sue does not mention her children, she engages with Jane and they build a good relationship over the next few weeks. Sue builds enough trust in Jane to disclose about her children and how her problem is affecting them. Jane explains that she can receive support from social services to help her manage. She makes a referral to social services with Sue's consent. She continues to provide support for Sue and social services provide some other wrap-around support.

Ethics and confidentiality

Whilst there are good legal reasons to maintain confidentiality, the real reason for a confidential service is for your client's benefit.

As a social care worker you will often be told or have access to deeply personal and private information about clients. You may know more about a client than their close friends or family. If clients are going to engage with you on an honest and open basis, they need to be reassured that what they tell you is kept confidential.

It is easy to forget quite how sensitive this issue can be for clients. Think of a piece of information that you hold very personal and would not like people to know about you. Imagine writing this information down on a piece of paper alongside your name, address, date of birth and telephone number. Put this piece of paper in an envelope and seal the envelope. Who would you feel comfortable giving this information to? How would you feel, knowing it was stored somewhere, that someone else could get access to that information? Having done this exercise in your head, make it real and write something on a piece of paper and see how it feels.

Many clients have good reason to want to keep their personal issues private, from family, from friends, from employers, from neighbours. They may not even want people to know that they are receiving support for a particular problem. Therefore you need to keep the fact that they are a client of yours confidential, as well as the information that they tell you. Many people outside of the social care professions are much more judgemental about personal problems than you may be. Even the simple fact of being in contact with a social care worker becoming public knowledge can be catastrophic.

Be careful who you tell

Worker: Jim, a counsellor

Client: Frank, who suffers from stress and anxiety

Jim has been seeing Frank for one-to-one sessions helping him deal with stress and anxiety brought on by his work in a bank and problems in his marriage. Neither Frank's wife nor his employers know that he is receiving counselling. They meet every Tuesday at 5.30 at Jim's office.

One Monday evening Jim's wife goes into labour. Not wanting Frank to travel all the way across town for a session that is unlikely to happen he leaves a message on Frank's phone. He does not receive a reply, so the next day he leaves a message with a colleague at Frank's work. In each message he identifies himself as Frank's counsellor.

Frank shares a mobile with his wife and she picks up the message. This makes his home life worse as his wife feels betrayed. The message at work was left with Frank's boss. The company is cutting its workforce and increasing the workload. Based on his knowledge about the counselling, Frank's boss worries that Frank won't be able to handle the pace and decides to let him go.

For us to be able to do our work properly and for clients to benefit fully from our services, they must feel comfortable disclosing personal information. If they don't feel comfortable they will probably not engage with the service in the first place. When a client is sitting with you, their focus should be on the issue that they are discussing. If they are worrying about who may find out what they are saying, or they are holding back from you because of this worry, they will not be getting the most out of their time with you.

In our favour there is a long history of confidentiality in social care services and clients expect to receive a confidential service. This means that, for the most part, if you reassure them that that the service you are providing is confidential then you can gain their trust. The long line of social care workers, doctors and priests stretching back in time who have maintained confidentiality have provided us with a steady platform to work from. However, this also places an extra weight of responsibility on us to maintain this tradition.

Find out who's asking

Worker: Ted, a street outreach worker

Client: Jane, a long term rough sleeper who has been refusing help from services for the last five years

Ted gets to know Jane over a nine-month period, initially building a relationship with her by helping her to get some medical treatment for her dog when it was ill. Ted manages to get Jane to tell him the out-of-the-way places she likes to sleep. She starts to come into the day centre once a week and slowly starts to open up to Ted about her past and how she ended up on the streets. He persuades her to see a doctor about a number of serious medical problems she has refused to deal with previously. Other workers and services are amazed at the progress as none of them were able to get Jane to engage with them at all.

One day a couple of clients come in who have known Jane for many years. They say that they are worried about her health and ask if Ted has seen her recently. He says that he saw her only last night behind a certain office block.

The clients find Jane, who owed them some money, in what she considered a safe and hidden place. They beat her and take her possessions, but not before telling her how they found her.

Jane stops coming to the day centre, moves out of the area and swears never to get involved with those 'do gooders' again.

Be aware, though, that even though you may get a basic level of trust from a client as they start to engage with you, it is very common for clients to hold back information until they build up a level of personal trust in you. As time progresses they will build up that trust, and may even test your level of confidentiality with a minor issue before bringing a major issue to you. It is therefore important that you maintain very clear confidentiality at all times. A minor slip may have a major impact on your future work with the client.

Testing the water

Worker: Sue, a floating support worker

Client: Clare, an 18-year-old young woman who has recently left the care system

Clare and Sue have been working together for about 6 months helping Clare settle into a new flat, and look after her two-year-old son. Clare is happy to be independent but still a little scared by the responsibility. Her boyfriend, who she has been with for eight months, has recently started to get violent and physically abusive towards her and her son. Sue knows it is not right but is scared that she will look like a bad mother in the eyes of social services if it comes out.

Clare tells Sue that she used to smoke cannabis on a regular basis before she had her son. Sue talks to her about it, checks that she does not smoke it any more, checks that there is none kept in the house and tells Clare that as long as she believes both these things are true she will not have to tell anyone. She reminds her of the confidentiality policy and they talk about the dangers of smoking cannabis around her son or if she is caring for him. They talk about what social services might be concerned about and what support they might provide.

A couple of weeks later, based on this positive experience Clare decides to tell Sue what has been happening with her boyfriend.

If a client is under the impression that you were going to keep something confidential that in fact you were obliged to share with outside parties, it could ruin your relationship. Make sure you have fully explained your confidentiality policy to clients before you start any work. If a client starts to disclose something that you may have to break confidentiality on then it may be worth stopping them and reminding them of the policy before they divulge too much.

Confidentiality in practice

Ensuring that you maintain confidentiality is not just about who you do or don't tell certain bits of information to.

Information relating to criminal acts

In the UK you *do not* have an obligation to break confidentiality just because it relates to a criminal matter. You do still have a duty of confidentiality to your client even if they have committed criminal acts. For countries outside the UK, check with your local professional association for further guidance on this matter.

You do not have to disclose information to the police if they ask you; you can request that they get a court order. However, if a court orders you to do so then you must disclose the information.

If the police do ask you for information then you can disclose it without breaking the Data Protection Act if you believe that it will prevent or detect crime or help prosecute or catch a suspect. You still have a duty to ensure that the information is to be used to prevent or detect a specific crime and will be used for the stated purpose. For more information relating to the UK see the website of the Information Commissioner (see Appendix II, 'Further Reading').

The criminal justice system

There are some social care roles that are intrinsically bound up with the criminal justice system, probation workers being a prime example. In these roles the level of confidentiality can vary. Increasingly other professions, particularly in the drugs field, are being linked in with the criminal justice system. If you are working with someone who has a court order, or are assessing them for court in some way, then the confidentiality boundaries will be radically different from those described above. In terms of professional boundaries this is not in itself a problem; however, you do need to be very clear with the client about the exact nature of your confidentiality or lack of it. (See Appendix II, 'Further Reading'.)

Mental capacity

Adults and children have a basic right to a confidential service and confidential treatment. However, there are times when you can override this right. You can break confidentiality if you believe that the individual concerned does not have the mental capacity (ability) to understand:

- the implications of the treatment that they are consenting to
- the implications of not consenting
- the nature or consequences of the issues that they are disclosing
- their own reasons for not disclosing to the relevant responsible adult.

The purpose of breaking confidentiality would be to speak to someone who has responsibility for the individual to inform them or get their consent.

When dealing with children, the 'Gillick Principles' apply. These are a set of guidelines developed in 1985 in relation to providing advice about contraception to young girls. They have become the standard guidelines to use when assessing whether a child can receive a confidential service.

For a fuller explanation of mental capacity see Chapter 7, 'Professional Boundaries and the Law'.

Confidentiality waivers

There are of course times when it is useful for both you and the client to share information with others; other professionals or members of the family are most common. It is very easy to get the client to sign a form which allows you to share information with named individuals or named organisations. Be sure that you are very clear with the client about what level of information you can share and make sure that the information is easily available to both you and anyone else in your team who may need it. If you are off sick, information may be requested and other members of staff need to know how to deal with it. If you have a large caseload then it can be hard to remember exactly what each client has specified.

Storage of information (hard/paper copy)

In theory we have enough technology to work in a 'paperless office'. But go into any social care office and the number of files, reports, forms and folders stuffed with paper will soon counteract that idea. Most of us have reams of paper on, by or about our clients, much of it containing confidential information.

This information needs to be in locked storage in a secure environment, which is simple enough to achieve in most cases. Do make sure that you think about who does and does not have access to the locked cabinets/room that you use (cleaners, volunteers, other professionals, etc.).

However, once we start a busy work day things can get more complicated. You need to be very careful what you do with every single piece of client paperwork that you have. Look at the short examples below and think about the harm that could be caused by some very simple slips:

- You leave a client file open on the desk in the open plan staff office where clients are not allowed. A policeman comes for a meeting with your boss. Whilst waiting for him to get off the phone the policeman sits in the chair at your desk and glances at your file.

- You leave a meeting with a client at their house carrying the paperwork from the session. A neighbour stops you to chat about the weather. A typed report for social services on headed paper is face-up on the outside of the bundle of papers you are carrying.

- Your client says that they would like a look at their file. In line with the Data Protection Act you have a meeting with them where they get to see all the paperwork. As they look at the notes they place one part of the assessment form by their feet and it ends up under the chair. You end the meeting leaving the paper under the chair.

- After a social service core group meeting at the end of the day across town from your office you go straight to meet a friend for a couple of drinks after work. You take care to keep the files zipped in an inside compartment of your bag. Whilst in the pub your bag gets stolen.

Storage of information (soft/digital copy)

If you are storing any information on a computer or other electronic format you must ensure that there is enough security and encryption to keep the data safe, particularly if you are going to carry a laptop, memory stick or information on CD. If a computer is shared by more than one person then you need to be especially careful. It is your professional responsibility to ensure that this data is safe. If you don't know enough about computers then you need to get an IT professional to help you.

Transmitting information

If you are going to send any confidential information through the post, by fax or over the internet you need to think carefully about the implications for confidentiality. Generally the best way to transmit information confidentially is by fax, by secure email or on the phone. Do make sure you know the fax machine is in a confidential location or that the other person has secure emails.

If you put a lot of confidential information in the post it could easily end up in the wrong hands, and normal emails can be hacked.

If you have no other choice but to post or email information, consider if you can anonymise the information by using initials and not putting addresses or dates of birth.

Clients seeing files

Clients do have a right to see everything that is recorded about them. However, you should not just hand the file over and leave them to it. If a client sees their file it should be with a worker present. This prevents any tampering with the contents of the file but also allows you to explain anything that the client does not understand or disagrees with.

As a result, it is sensible to have a policy relating to clients seeing files that they should request a viewing in advance. This allows you to book some time to spend with them as they look at the file.

Seeing clients walk down the street

If you see a client walking down the street, even by acknowledging them you could be breaching confidentiality. They may be with someone who starts asking who you are. Other members of the public or the people they are with may know that you are a social care professional and jump to conclusions. From the point of view of confidentiality the best bet is to ignore them. However, they may see this as cold or aloof behaviour and take it negatively. Best practice is to wait and see if they notice you and how they respond. If they put their head down and carry on then do the same; however, if they wave and shout hello then they clearly don't have any problem and you can respond appropriately.

Public places

There are many times when you will be in public with staff or clients and a confidential subject may come up. It is very easy to come out of a meeting with a client, or with other professionals, and to stand on the street continuing a conversation that started inside. You may end up going for a coffee with a fellow team member whilst waiting for a bus, or you could be chatting with that same team member on the bus. Be careful about the conversations that you have, as you never know who might be listening. The bus driver may be your client's cousin, the waiter could be their father, a client may pass by and hear you talking about them or other clients.

Be aware also of the tone of conversation that you use. Even if all the details of a story are carefully anonymised, to the ears of an outsider it may be shocking to hear care workers discussing people's cases.

Phone enquiries

It is quite common for someone to call up asking for information on a client. Often it is another professional after information. Never give out information unless you have looked at the client's file to check if they have signed a waiver for information to be shared with this person or service. You should also be careful that the person on the other end of the phone is who they say they are. It would be very easy for someone to claim to be a social worker or probation officer. If you are not sure, you can always call them back on a recognised landline number to ensure that they are genuine.

Contacting clients

Be aware that by phoning and leaving a message or sending a letter you may be compromising your client's confidentiality. Do not have envelopes marked with your organisation's name or field of business, do mark envelopes as private and confidential, and check with clients in advance whether they are happy for you to contact them by post at the address they have given you. When leaving phone messages for clients make sure that you leave as little information as possible about who you are, where you are calling from and why you are calling.

Chapter 6

Beginnings and Endings

Starting and ending relationships

The beginning and end of a relationship are very powerful moments and can have a deep impact on the outcome of your interaction with your client. Therefore it is important to ensure that both the start and finish of a relationship are managed properly. There are a number of practical and emotional areas to consider. The issues to consider at the start are more practical and relate to setting the tone and managing client expectations. Towards the end of the relationship the issues are more emotional but you also need to consider move-on and onward referrals.

Some relationships have clearly defined time limits and fixed beginning and end points, which make managing this process easier (e.g. one-to-one support sessions with a client for ten weeks). However, many workers will be engaging with clients on a more random basis (e.g. in a day centre, on the street, as one member of a large team with many clients), or may have relationships brought to a premature end by a client failing to attend sessions or by other external constraints.

The guidelines in this chapter should be followed wherever possible, but where necessary you should apply them as closely as appropriate, or possible, given your situation.

Beginnings

First impressions count – the start of a relationship sets the tone and can create patterns of behaviour and assumptions that will impact on how the relationship progresses. Most of us make a judgement very quickly about people we meet, and then look for behaviour that meets or justifies this judgement.

When a client first meets you or one of your team, how are they greeted, how much time are they given, what impression to they get? Sometimes something as little as a welcoming smile, a handshake and some good eye contact can be enough to get a wary client to relax and engage.

The first meeting is a chance for the worker to get to know the client, create expectations and to lay out you have to offer. It is also a chance for the client to decide whether the service that you offer is right for them.

When preparing to meet a client you should:

- *Get information from other agencies or workers.* In some situations you will have access to referral forms, risk assessments or other written information or you can call relevant agencies/ workers. Having information in advance can help you speed up the process and work more effectively. Be aware, though, that the information you are given may be subjective.

- *Ensure that you have the correct paperwork and information with you.* Being prepared and organised saves time and ensures the smooth running of the session. It also gives a good first impression and allows both you and the client to concentrate on the session.

- *Review any information that you have on a client.* If you have been given information, make sure you are aware of its contents. If there is key information that you have not been given and you realise it too late it can cause problems for you or the client. Be careful not to make judgements or assumptions based on the information that you receive.

At the start of the relationship you should:

- *Explain the aim or purpose of the relationship/service, and your role as a worker.* Clients may not understand what it is that you do and what they can get from you. For example, they may mistake a key worker for a counsellor, or may think that you will help support them in areas that you are not able to.

- *Tell them the length of each session, the expected length of the relationship/service and any review periods.* It is important for clients to understand the time limits so that it does not come as a shock to them when the session/service ends. It also allows them to make better judgements about when to divulge information, and when to start preparing themselves for the ending.

- *Explain carefully and clearly the level of confidentiality that you can offer.* If the client does not understand what you will and won't keep confidential, then you can lose the client's trust if you have to share information when they were expecting it to stay between the two of you.

- *Explain any rules or expectations you have of their behaviour, and consequences for not abiding by them (if applicable).* Clients may not realise what are the implications of their behaviour, for you or for them. If you do not explain any rules or expectations to them, then it is harder and unfair if they are then penalised. It is worth explaining really basic boundaries such as attending on time, acceptable behaviour towards staff and other clients, not attending under the influence of substances and appropriate use of language.

- *Allow the client to ask any questions.* Many clients will have concerns or worries about the service, and it is important that they get a chance to address these concerns. Make sure that you leave enough time for them to ask questions as part of the session so that you do not have to run over time to answer them. Clients may be confused about, or unaware of, these areas. If you do not take the chance to clearly explain them, you may be setting your client up for disappointment at a later stage in the relationship when it does not meet their expectations.

Endings

Almost all professional relationships will necessarily have a clear end point, unlike friendships or personal relationships. When a professional relationship ends it is important to ensure that there is a clear sense of ending, that the emotions involved are dealt with appropriately and that there is a sensible and well thought out move-on or follow-up process. A bad ending can be emotionally damaging to the client and cause problems for future professional relationships and may undo good work that has been done.

Many people have difficulty ending relationships appropriately or dealing with the emotions brought up by the ending. When a meaningful relationship ends, the individuals involved may go through a process of grieving and may experience all the emotions and processes involved in the grief process. Elizabeth Kübler-Ross describes five stages of the grief process: denial, anger, bargaining, depression and acceptance. You or your client may experience any or all of the processes, although not necessarily in the order described.

It is also common for ending to bring up feelings of loss and abandonment. This is true for both workers and clients and is therefore twice as difficult to deal with. Don't underestimate the impact that the ending of a relationship may have on either you or your clients.

If you have had a long or meaningful relationship with a client then you will have built up a bond and the client in particular may have a lot invested in the relationship. They may have come to rely not only on the service that they have received, but on you as an individual, or the general support that they receive from attending the sessions/service.

Many people do not like dealing with the interaction involved with ending a relationship and may avoid a final session so as not to deal with the process. Some people have very bad experiences of ending previous relationships and will bring their feelings or experience to ending other relationships. It is also very common for individuals to not want to end relationships and to hang on to a relationship longer than is necessary. As a worker it may be difficult for you to let go of the relationship with the client.

The end of a relationship is when any symptoms of over-dependence (see Chapter 9, 'Understanding Negative Consequences') may surface and it is important that they are dealt with appropriately.

Before the end of a relationship you should:

- *Set up follow-on support/services.* Many clients will need other services or ongoing support after they finish their time with you. Make sure that you have discussed this well in advance and have made suitable referrals with enough time so that the client is not left waiting too long without any support. Not all clients require follow-on support and they should be allowed to choose if they need or want any further support.

- *Manage the transfer to other workers smoothly.* If you are leaving the service and your client is going to work with another worker at the same service, you should give them plenty of warning, introduce them to the new worker and have a three-way handover meeting.

- *Warn clients if the relationship is going to end, with enough time to process their feelings.* You may have told them at the start when the relationship is going to end, but they may have forgotten or misinterpreted what you said. Make sure that the ending/final session does not come as a shock to them.

- *Allow the client a chance to discuss their feelings on the ending of the relationship/service.* Clients may not bring this up themselves and it is important that you ask them about their feelings. Their reaction could be anything from very emotional to total denial that they have any feelings about it. Be prepared for a negative or aggressive reaction from some clients who have had previous bad experiences or who cannot process their emotions about the ending suitably.

- *Acknowledge your own feelings about the ending of the relationship.* You do not need to come across as cold and unfeeling and you can acknowledge in a professional manner that you have feelings about the end of the relationship. Be careful not to allow your emotions to dominate the time you have with the client.

- *Review the outcome of the relationship.* Discussing what has been achieved, and what changes have been made, not only helps clients see how far they have come but can help move along the process of ending the relationship.

- *Consider how you feel about the ending of the relationship.* Whilst your feelings should not be the main focus of any time you spend with the client, it is important that you understand and acknowledge your own feelings.

- *Establish clearly whether or not the client can re-contact you or the re-use the service.* Over-dependent clients may keep trying to see you or use the service even after the end of a relationship, while other clients may feel that they are not welcome back even though they are. It is important to establish this clearly with the client.

After a relationship has ended:

- *Do not establish a personal relationship with the client.* Once you have had a professional relationship with a client it is unethical to continue to have a personal relationship with them, whether it is a simple friendship or a sexual relationship. It will often be against policy and procedure within your organisation. Ongoing personal relationships may look very suspicious to other clients and professionals, will increase a sense of blurred boundaries and can damage good work done within a professional capacity.

- *Do not continue working with the client, formally or informally.* If you have ended the relationship, it is not appropriate to continue to provide support services to the client on a formal or informal basis unless this is within the remit of your service and job description. There is a strong chance of an increasing dependency upon you as an individual if you do provide support yourself. Working as part of an organisation/service provides many safety nets for a client in terms of supervision and continuity of service. Providing a service outside of these structures can set you or your client up for future difficulties.

- *Do not maintain contact with the client.* Clients may want to ring you or pop in to see you. Whilst you can speak to them if necessary, do ensure that they don't start to use you as a support or a crutch. If they do contact you regularly you need to let them know that it is not appropriate and refer them to other more suitable support services. It may be tempting to contact a client to see how they are doing; however, doing this opens the door for them to start contacting you and implies that you wish the relationship to continue and should be avoided.

- *Do not have another professional relationship with the client.* If your client is an electrician/pensions adviser or in another profession that is useful to you, it may be tempting to make use of their services. This is also unethical and can lead to many complications. It may be possible that you can offer other professional services to the client outside of your previous support role; this also falls into the same category.

Explain your expectations

Jill is a key worker in a hostel for homeless clients and has been assigned to work with a new arrival, Dee. During her first session with Dee she explains that she will see him for one hour every two weeks whilst he is staying at the hostel and that the purpose of the sessions is to discuss his progress and deal with any problems he is having. She completes a basic assessment form, explains about meal times, staffing levels, curfew times and rules about guests at the hostel, asks if Dee has any questions and books in their next appointment in two weeks' time.

At their next appointment Dee turns up late and intoxicated and Jill gives him a warning, which Dee is not happy about.

During their third session Dee tells Jill that his children are being physically abused by his ex-partner, but that he does not want to tell anyone because he does not want the children taken into care. Jill says she is obliged to inform social services about this information. Dee becomes abusive and aggressive, saying he thought she would keep things secret for him. He gets a second and final warning about his behaviour.

Over the next couple of months Dee and Jill build up their relationship more positively and Dee starts to open up to her and access other support services that she suggests. He is slowly turning his life around, with Jill's help.

Jill applies for and gets a promotion to another hostel. She tells Dee in his next session that this will be her last session with him and that she will have to pass him over to another worker, though she is not sure who it will be. Dee becomes very angry, saying that Jill is just like all the other workers, she doesn't really care about him and that they have been wasting their time. He smashes his chair into a window in the door and storms out. As he is already on his final warning, Dee is evicted from the hostel due to his behaviour.

Jill is not responsible for Dee's behaviour. However, if she had clearly explained her expectations for him to be on time and sober during key work, laid out the confidentiality policy clearly and given Dee some warning that she might be leaving, then it is possible that Dee may still be in the hostel and on track.

Questions to think about

- How do you deal with endings in your personal life, when you leave a job or end a personal relationship?

- How good are you at remembering everything that needs to be covered in a session with a client?

- How responsible are you for what happens to a client after the end of a relationship?

- How would you feel explaining to a long-term client that you are unable to continue working with them due to funding cuts?

- If you bumped into a client in the street and their life was clearly not heading in a positive direction since your relationship ended, what would you do and how would you feel?

Chapter 7

Professional Boundaries and the Law

There is a wide variety of legislation that relates or links to professional boundaries. There is an even greater number of guidance and implementation documents. This book focuses primarily on law within the UK, but other countries will have similar structures and ethical frameworks.

This chapter provides a guide to the main pieces of UK legislation that have the most impact on social care workers' day-to-day practice in relation to professional boundaries. It is not a complete guide to the law in relation to the social care sector. If you are running an organisation or your own practice then there are many more implications for your practice than are mentioned in this chapter.

The key professional boundary in relation to the law is your responsibility to know the relevant laws and official guidance relating to your line of work. Ignorance or lack of training is no excuse – it is very easy to do some research and find out the relevant legislation. Your professional duty is to ensure that you are up-to-date and informed of relevant legal issues.

If you are outside of the UK your local professional associations will advise you on local laws and best practice.

Relevant legislation

The key relevant Acts in this context are as follows.

Mental Health Act

These Acts cover the powers to detain individuals for their own safety or the safety of the public:

- *Mental Health Act 1983*
- *Mental Health (Scotland) Act 1984*
- *Mental Health (Detention) Scotland) Act 1991*
- *Mental Health (Public Safety and Appeals) (Scotland) Act 1999*
- *Mental Health (Care and Treatment) (Scotland) Act 2003.*

Human Rights Act

These enshrine individuals' human rights in British Law:

- *Human Rights Act 1998*
- *Scottish Commission for Human Rights Act 2006.*

Data Protection Act 1998

This Act provides regulation of how personal/confidential information and information about public services is managed. (For more information see Chapter 5, 'Confidentiality'.)

Domestic Violence, Crime and Victims Act 2004

This Act created a specific offence of 'causing or allowing the death of a child or vulnerable adult'.

Mental Capacity Act 2005

This Act brings together previous laws and best practice on assessing mental capacity and dealing with individuals who have been judged not have the capacity to make decisions for themselves.

Safeguarding Vulnerable Groups Act 2006 and Protection of Vulnerable Groups (Scotland) Act 2007

These Acts set up a system of vetting and barring of individuals working with children and vulnerable adults and place obligations for monitoring and disclosure of abuse of these groups.

✧

In most areas of social care we have to respect clients' wishes and boundaries, even if we don't like or approve of what they are doing. However, there are two key exceptions to this, described below.

'Sectioning' / forced detention

The Mental Health Act 1983 makes allowances for people to be forcibly detained in hospital and in some situations forcibly treated. This book covers what is commonly known as 'sectioning' as this is what the majority of social care professionals encounter in their day-to-day work.

'Being sectioned' or 'sectioning' refers to keeping people with a 'mental disorder' in a specialist hospital for their safety or the safety of the general public. It is referred to as 'sectioning' because there are a number of different methods and reasons for detaining people and each one has its own section in the Mental Health Act.

Whilst there are a number of different sections, the key facts are that someone who is judged to be a risk to themselves and others can be 'sectioned' (forcibly detained in a mental health institution) for anything up to six months. For emergency detentions of up to 72 hours this decision can be made by one doctor, for longer periods the decision needs to be made by two doctors.

As a social care professional, if you believe that one of your clients presents a risk to themselves or to other people then you can request an assessment. If it is an emergency then contact the police. If there is no need for immediate action then you can contact your local social services or mental health trust.

A full breakdown of the implications of the Act can be found on the Mind website (see Appendix II, 'Further Reading').

Mental capacity

Adults and children have a basic right to a confidential service and to consent to their own treatment, assuming that they have the 'mental capacity' to understand and communicate about it. This has an important impact on client confidentiality. It also introduces a new set of boundaries that you have to work within if your client lacks capacity.

The Mental Capacity Act 2005 sets out five key principles:

1. A person must be assumed to have capacity unless it is established that he lacks capacity.

2. A person is not to be treated as unable to make a decision unless all practicable steps to help him to do so have been taken without success.

3. A person is not to be treated as unable to make a decision merely because he makes an unwise decision.

4. An act done, or decision made, under this Act for or on behalf of a person who lacks capacity must be done, or made, in his best interests.

5. Before the act is done, or the decision is made, regard must be had to whether the purpose for which it is needed can be as effectively achieved in a way that is less restrictive of the person's rights and freedom of action.

If a client is judged not to have mental capacity, then someone, or an official body, needs to take responsibility for taking decisions for them. Decisions cannot be taken in isolation and all relevant carers, professionals and family members need to be consulted.

If you are not fully trained and you have an issue that you believe requires a capacity assessment then you should contact your line manager immediately. There are professional assessors available to consult with you and advise you.

The assessment may lead you to believe that the individual concerned *does not have* the mental capacity (ability) to understand:

- the implications of the treatment that they are consenting to

- the implications of not consenting

- the nature or consequences of the issues that they are disclosing

- their own reasons for not disclosing to the relevant responsible adult.

If so, you must find someone who has been given Power of Attorney over the individual, a parent if the individual is under 18, or go to the Court of Protection who manage individual cases.

There are many reasons why someone might be judged not to have capacity, based on their mental or learning ability, their age, whether they are intoxicated, and their state of mind. However, you should not make assumptions or judgements about whether someone has the capacity to consent. You must make a full and reasoned assessment. It is also important to note that disagreeing with your professional opinion is not grounds for assessing someone as not having capacity.

To judge someone as competent you have to be convinced that they can:

- understand information that they are given

- retain information long enough to make a decision

- weigh up the information to help make the decision

- communicate the outcome of their decision.

It is important to understand that mental capacity/competency changes over time and from issue to issue. It is not a matter of deciding that someone is not competent to consent to anything ever again. Each decision must be judged on its merits. You may, for example, decide that someone is competent to receive confidential advice and information, but not to consent to an in-depth medical procedure. If someone is very drunk you could judge them not competent to consent to anything; however, when they are sober they could have full mental capacity to consent to everything.

This does raise some difficult issues when you are working with clients with recurring mental health problems. When someone is in the grip of their illness they may have a very different viewpoint from when their mental health is stable. This can create a wildly fluctuating competency which is hard to manage whilst respecting the client's wishes at different times.

Whilst the Mental Capacity Act is not designed to provide guidance for working with children generally, roughly the same principles apply. When working with young people (under 18) it is generally assumed that you should involve their parents and get their parents' permission for any serious intervention. If you or the young person believe that there is good reason not to involve their parents, you can only do so if the person is judged to have the capacity to understand and consent to the intervention.

For further information on mental capacity and the law, see Appendix II, 'Further Reading'.

Safeguarding adults and children

Safeguarding legislation and guidance is essentially designed to ensure that children and vulnerable adults are protected from abuse and harm. It is an area that has grown and changed hugely in the last ten years across the world and is also an area that is having a massive impact on the social care system.

In the UK a combination of the Safeguarding Vulnerable Groups Act and a government guidance document 'No Secrets' (Department of Health 2000) introduced a new level of professional expectations for social care workers.

The area is currently it is referred to as safeguarding, though it has previously been known as protecting. It will no doubt change again and the exact procedures may change. However, the basic concepts will not change any time soon and should still apply, therefore this book covers the concept generally without going into too much detail about process and procedure. You will find that most countries outside the UK have a similar system in place.

Reading this section is not sufficient for you to know or understand fully about dealing with safeguarding issues. Make sure that you get more in-depth training and support around the issue.

Vulnerable adults

'Vulnerable adults' has a specific meaning in terms of the legislation. It applies to people who receive social care or are in supported accommodation as a result of a mental or physical disability or health problem, addictions, or anything else that reduces their mental or physical ability, and are dependent on others for their basic care or unable to protect or defend themselves from others.

Safeguarding children

For the purposes of safeguarding, anyone up to 18 years old is a child.

You must ensure that you understand your local organisation's policies and procedures relating to safeguarding. If you work alone then you must understand local procedures for alerting and have some procedures in place for yourself.

❖

The idea that we have to protect children from abuse is widely understood and accepted. However, it is only in recent years that we have realised that vulnerable adults also suffer from abuse and need to be protected in similar ways.

Whilst there are particular elements of dealing with vulnerable adults and children that are different, the underpinning processes and how they impact on us as social care workers are essentially the same.

Reports and enquiries into the deaths of children and vulnerable adults have found a number of problems with the social care system that meant that it was failing many vulnerable adults and children in its care. There are a number of problems that have been identified:

- Agencies had information about the situation that was not shared with the relevant authorities.

- Agencies with responsibility to keep children and vulnerable adults safe were failing to address the needs of these individuals and keep them safe.

- There was not a comprehensive system of vetting and barring staff, and potentially dangerous individuals were free to work for new organisations after abusing people in the past.

A more comprehensive system of checks and registers was introduced, although this system has changed since and will no doubt change again. However, the big change in terms of professional boundaries is that:

Anyone engaged in social care must take responsibility for watching out for and reporting signs of abuse.

This means that whether you are a mental health practitioner, a home care worker or hostel manager, you have a duty to report on any signs of abuse of children or vulnerable adults, whether the individuals concerned are directly in your care or not. If you overhear a conversation about something suspicious, you have a duty to report it. You also have a duty to try to follow up your report to check what has happened as a result.

This essentially places a new professional obligation (boundary) on all social care workers and one that may not relate to the main focus of your work. It is very easy to assume that someone else knows about it and therefore something is being done, or that because the client has a social worker then you have no responsibility for the issue.

It is your responsibility to ensure that you fully understand the different forms of abuse and the signs and symptoms of abuse. If you do not have training on this, ensure that you get some, either through your employer or privately.

Make sure that you are not the one person who knew what was going on and didn't tell anyone. Don't make any assumptions about who knows what and who is doing what. You may only be dealing with one part of the picture, but unless you share information you will never know if you are dealing with the most important part, or hold a key piece of information that may assist someone else. If you have suspicions then you should contact your local social services or the police (depending on how urgent a response you need and how serious the issue is).

The other area highlighted by the investigations is that a series of errors, omissions and slipped boundaries by a number of professionals and organisations contributed to the deaths. Lots of small slips and lost opportunities by lots of people add up to a big problem. Don't become part of the problem. Stay focused and professional with your own work as well as keeping an eye out for safeguarding issues.

Equal opportunities

Equality of opportunity is an area that is now enshrined in law, and it is illegal to discriminate against individuals on the grounds of race/ ethnicity, gender, age, sexuality, ability or belief.

From a professional social care perspective there are many good reasons to work in an anti-discriminatory way. To be anti-discriminatory is to treat everyone fairly, not make assumptions and to try our best to meet everyone's needs. All of these things are good practice to make clients feel safe, welcomed and to avoid building resentment and hostility. However, the legislation makes it a more legally binding matter than just good practice.

It is vital that as many potential clients as possible are able to access the service that you provide. This means that they have to know about the service, be able to physically access the service, should feel comfortable, safe and welcomed and not discriminated against once they are there and there should be no obvious barriers to their accessing the service.

Once people do access your service it is important that they feel comfortable about themselves and their background. This means that you should not tolerate any discriminatory language or behaviour on any grounds from any member of staff or client. It is important that this behaviour is not accepted and is firmly challenged.

On an organisational level equality of opportunity has a massive impact in terms of employment, publicity, monitoring and policy and procedure. For the worker on the ground it also has a wide range of implications. Most of these are contained implicitly in the basic boundaries that you will find in this book, but there are two that are worth mentioning specifically:

- *Publicising the service.* It is important that you think about all the potential client groups that you might want to reach and how you can get the message to them that your service exists. You may need to think about advertising in new ways, in new places or in new languages.

- *Access.* There are obvious access issues such as wheelchair access to consider, but you should also think about where your service is based, when it is open and how easy it is for people to arrive at your service without being identified with a particular client group (e.g. an obvious needle exchange programme next to a school is unlikely to attract parents from that school).

It is worth pointing out that providing equality of access or equality of treatment is not 'treating everyone the same'. If you had a blind client you would offer them extra support to engage with the service, help in finding their way around, help in reading any paperwork that could not be provided in Braille, and so on. This is an obvious example of treating people differently so that they can receive the same service.

What does need to be the same is that they are offered the same opportunities. It is very easy to make assumptions about people based on their race/ethnicity, gender, age, sexuality, ability or belief and to not include clients in certain activities or not to offer them the same opportunities as everyone else.

In terms of day-to-day practice you need to ensure that you assess everyone's needs, meet those needs wherever possible and practical, and treat everyone as an individual.

Questions to think about

- What are the specific laws that apply to your particular sector/job?

- What government guidance has been issued that has an impact on your work?

If you don't know, do some research.

Chapter 8

Broken Boundaries

A boundary crossing (or broken boundary) occurs when a worker or a client acts, or even thinks, in a way that clearly steps across the line of acceptable behaviour.

A social care professional needs to ensure that they keep their own behaviour within acceptable boundaries, but they also need to ensure that their client's behaviour also stays within acceptable limits.

It is important to have a good understanding of what happens when boundaries are crossed. As a worker you have to make frequent, off-the-cuff, decisions as you are working, often in difficult or pressured situations requiring an instant response.

This chapter analyses the decision-making processes and judgements that social care workers make all day, every day. This will involve going into a great deal of detail. However, whilst it is important to be able to analyse your decisions and actions, you can not and should not analyse everything you do in as much detail as is done here.

Understanding and analysing situations becomes easier as you gain more knowledge of the client group that you are working with, the setting that you are working in and the particular clients that you work with. The more experienced you are, the easier and quicker you will find dealing with boundary issues.

Boundaries crossings are inevitable when working in most social care settings. Even with the most diligent boundaries management and very focused work, boundaries will get crossed at some point or other. The measure of a good worker is spotting them soon enough and dealing with them effectively.

Reasons for boundary crossings

Boundary crossings occur for a variety of reasons:

- *As a result of an action by a worker.* This could be the result of forgetfulness or a mistake, poor training, poor decision-making, lack of information, a deliberate but well intentioned decision, or in some cases a malicious and intentioned piece of boundary breaking and abuse.

- *As a result of an action by a client.* Through lack of understanding of boundaries, an inability to keep within boundaries, intoxication or a deliberate breaking of boundaries.

- *Accidentally.* There are many situations where a boundary can be crossed through no fault of the worker or client. For example, they both visit the same pub/club on the same night, or both get invited to the same wedding.

- *Organisational failure/negligence.* Mismanagement, lack of funds or lack of staff can all lead to boundaries being crossed.

No one is perfect

We are all human and make mistakes. When working in social care we have to make complex judgements balancing up many factors in a short space of time. It is inevitable that mistakes or bad judgement calls will happen even with experienced workers.

Time and stress

Many social care workers have a high volume of paperwork, too large a caseload and not enough time. It is easy to forget a small detail or to leave something out when you are stressed and pressured, or in some cases there may just not be enough time in the day to do everything that is required of you. This is not an excuse for boundary breaking, but it is a reality that these pressures will lead to boundaries being broken.

Communication

Unfortunately many teams find it difficult to communicate sufficiently between themselves to make sure they have enough information to manage boundaries consistently. This is often due to pressures on time and workload and the sheer volume of information that would need to be communicated to keep on top of everything.

Different approaches/personalities

Within a team or an organisation there is likely to be a wide range of personalities and approaches to working with clients. This is beneficial to clients as different clients will be suited to different ways of working. However, it can make it challenging to manage and enforce boundaries in a uniform and consistent way.

Challenging roles and settings

Many of the roles and settings that social care workers find themselves in, place them in a very difficult position with regard to boundaries. The nature of their job or parts of their role means that they are automatically in a grey area, for example:

- *Floating support workers, or home care workers, work closely with clients in their own homes.* When working in someone else's home the boundaries are much more blurred than when you are in a 'work' setting.

- *Hostel or day centre workers can spend a lot of time, over an extended period, with clients that is not directly therapeutic or focused.* This can lead to more social interaction and a closer, more personal, relationship.

- *If you work in a small local community you are much more likely to see your clients outside of work.* They will know more about you and it will be harder to avoid dual relationships.

- *In a majority of social care roles, workers need to, and are encouraged to, build 'rapport' with their clients.* It is a very fine line between building rapport and over-stepping your boundaries and letting the relationship become more personal. The techniques that are commonly used for building rapport can easily give the client a sense that a personal or close relationship is being built.

Accidents happen

There will always be situations that arise unexpectedly that you could not have foreseen or prevented that lead to boundaries being crossed.

Client manipulation

Of course, not all clients are manipulative. However, many vulnerable groups have reasons to manipulate or play the system to their own advantage. Clients who have been institutionalised are particularly good at working the system, and if they have been in institutions since they were young may have had many more years' experience than the workers they are sitting opposite. With some client groups the relentless manipulation and pushing of boundaries makes it inevitable that some boundaries will get crossed.

Human interaction is complex

When you have two humans interacting on a deep level it is a very complex process and there are not always hard and fast lines to be drawn. Making boundary decisions based on the nuances of your personal relationship with a client is challenging and with the best will in the world it is possible to make the wrong call.

Assessing boundary crossings

If we are going to understand boundary crossings, it is useful to be able to grade how serious or harmful the crossings are. Traditionally, broken boundaries have been categorised as 'boundary crossings' and 'boundary violations'. However, this is too simplistic to gain a full understanding of what happens when boundaries are broken.

The crossing/violation model

Many boundary theories use the concept of boundary crossings and boundary violations. This idea is a convenient way to talk about and discuss boundaries, though it is not adequate to deal with the complexities of boundary issues and also not practical enough to help with day-to-day decision-making.

The idea is that *boundary crossings* are actions that are outside of standard professional actions but that do not cause direct harm. *Boundary violations* on the other hand are actions which cause direct harm. The general idea is that boundary crossings are manageable and likely to occur from time to time but that violations are much more serious and generally seen as unacceptable. Examples are:

- *Boundaried behaviour.* Being polite and respectful to clients, completing all paperwork correctly, challenging clients appropriately for racist language.

- *Boundary crossing.* Telling a client some minor personal information, being late for a session, forgetting to hand over all information at handover, not explaining boundaries clearly to a client, accepting a hug from a client.

- *Boundary violations.* Hitting a client, having sex with a client, major breaches of confidentiality.

In general discussion these terms are useful and allow us to communicate about boundaries in a simple manner, and to differentiate between more and less serious issues. However, for it to be a really useful tool we need to be able to decide accurately which category an action falls into and where to draw the line between the two categories.

In order to decide where to draw the line, you need to decide what it is that makes one incident more serious than another. The thing that makes one action more serious than another is the harm that it can, or may, cause.

We all understand that swearing in front of a client is not as serious as punching them in the face, but what about the host of other broken boundaries that range somewhere in between, and either side of these two extremes?

Assessing the amount of harm caused is complex and so we need a more fluid and complex system to assess broken boundaries.

The 'grey area' scale

The truth is that there is only boundaried and appropriate behaviour on the one hand, and inappropriate behaviour that has broken or crossed boundaries on the other. Once a boundary has been crossed it can have serious implications and needs to be dealt with before it becomes out of your control. The amount of harm that is caused can vary greatly, depending on a great number of factors.

To reflect this the 'grey area' model uses a sliding scale, which measures harm (potential or actual harm). It has safe, unharmful behaviour at one end, actions which cause serious harm at the other end and a graduated scale as the harm gets more serious as you move from one end to the other.

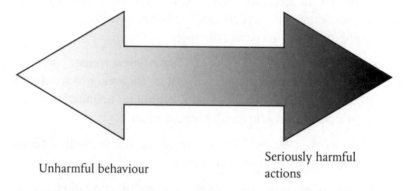

Unharmful behaviour

Seriously harmful actions

The literal, and metaphorical, 'grey area' represents the fluidity of the scale. How serious an action is will change depending on the situation, the worker and the client.

This scale is just a graphical representation of a theory about boundaries. As a worker you need a practical plan to apply the theory to your day-to-day work. The reality is that you need to spot boundary crossings when they occur and then react appropriately to manage the situation.

This can be broken into three distinct sections:

1. *Awareness.* To be able to deal with broken boundaries appropriately you need to spot that they have occurred. In the hustle and bustle of the working day whilst concentrating on your main purpose this is not always easy.

2. *Analysis.* Next you need to understand the implications and potential harm caused by the situation.

3. *Action.* Finally you need to take some corrective or preventative action to try to minimise any harm caused and prevent further broken boundaries.

1. Awareness

A good social care worker needs to be constantly keeping a check on both their own behaviour and emotions and those of their clients. This level of awareness of self and others is necessary for you to keep tabs on boundary issues whilst doing the rest of your job.

If you are not aware of boundary issues happening or building up then you will not be able to deal with them until they become so complex and entrenched that it is incredibly difficult to remedy the situation. If you only spot a build-up of boundary issues after a really serious incident, you are already too late. If you are unsure if a boundary has been crossed then treat it as if it has been crossed.

It is useful to look at boundary crossings in relation to your level of awareness of them. The reasons for the boundary crossing still fall into one of the four categories (worker action, client action, accidental, organisational), and the categories below can cross over. A boundary crossing may happen because of your subconscious but it becomes obvious as soon as it happens, or an obvious boundary crossing by a client may be a sign that alerts you to hidden boundary crossings.

ACTIVE BOUNDARY CROSSINGS

Some boundary crossings are very obvious because the action or situation clearly contravenes a boundary.

An active boundary crossing is one which involves an act or an act of omission by an individual: doing or saying something that you should not do or say, or not doing or saying what you should.

Most boundary crossings will involve a client or a worker behaving in an inappropriate way. These are all active boundary crossings: if a client hugs you, if you swear violently in front of a client, if a client turns up on your front doorstep.

You will spot these as soon as they happen and will be aware almost immediately that something is wrong. You should be able to take action straight away to deal with the problem, or at least decide on a course of action and put a plan into effect. A good understanding of basic boundaries will help you spot obvious boundary crossings.

EMOTIONAL BOUNDARY CROSSINGS

An emotional boundary crossing is one which occurs inside someone's head/heart/spirit (whichever you prefer). If a worker is sexually attracted to a client, or a client becomes dependent on a worker, then an emotional boundary has been crossed.

It is harder to spot emotional boundary crossings because they do not involve a physical action in themselves. However, they will manifest themselves as active boundary crossings.

So, to be aware of emotional boundary crossings you must look for signs or patterns of active boundary crossings that indicate that a boundary has been crossed:

- A client tells you that you are the only person who understands them – indicating that they are becoming dependent on you.

- You find yourself thinking about a client at home in the evening – indicating that you have become overly involved with the client and their issues.

Paying close attention to the subtle signals of speech and body language, and looking at the reasons for your client's obvious boundary crossings, will help you to spot emotional boundary crossings.

Unfortunately it is very common for us to lose sight of the bigger picture and get caught up in what is going on for us and for our client. We can very easily misinterpret our own behaviour and our judgement can become clouded.

JUSTIFYING BOUNDARY CROSSINGS

It is quite common to find workers justifying their actions to themselves and taking no action if they believe that the boundary crossing was justified. This is a classic error and one that should be avoided. The truth is that there are very few good reasons for boundaries to be crossed. Classic reasons that workers give for breaking boundaries include:

- It will build rapport.
- It will save a lot of time.
- The client really needs a break.
- If I just do this thing then everything will be sorted.
- The client won't manage if I don't.

In most situations the harm that occurs from a situation is the same whether the situation is entirely justified and understandable or not.

If you find yourself explaining (to yourself or others) why you are doing things differently, that this particular client is different or special or why this situation is different, then you are at the very least in a high-risk situation, and quite possibly have crossed a few boundaries.

If you are working in a boundaried way, then you will not need to justify or explain any of your actions to yourself or anyone else. It will be clear to you and other professionals that you are acting in the correct way.

We all talk to ourselves internally about our actions (self-talk) and to our colleagues about our clients. Keep an eye on how you talk to yourself and your colleagues. If you find yourself justifying actions, or avoiding talking about certain clients or situations, then you are probably breaking boundaries.

The damage is done

Let's say that a worker leaves a client's personal file lying around unattended in a communal area of a project. Other clients could pick up and read confidential information about the client. This could:

- cause embarrassment/shame for the client
- damage the relationship between the client and the worker/ project
- cause problems between the clients

- place the client in danger

- stop the client engaging with services.

The file could have been left there for all sorts of reasons:

- *Forgetfulness.* The worker just put it down and forgot to pick it up again.

- *An emergency.* A client had a heart attack in the foyer and the worker rushed to their aid leaving the file there.

- *Malicious action.* The worker may have purposefully left the file there so that someone could find it.

We would all condemn but understand the forgetful worker and they would probably get a reprimand from their manager. No one would blame the worker rushing to the aid of the client and they would not get disciplined at all. There is no justification for the malicious action by the worker and if it was discovered they would be severely disciplined.

However, whatever the reason, if clients do pick up the folder the damage caused will be the same. Once you have spotted that a boundary has been crossed, what matters is what you do next.

SUBCONSCIOUS BOUNDARY CROSSINGS

Subconscious boundary crossings occur when a worker is so caught up in their own issues or the client's issues that they are unaware that they are crossing any boundaries. It is mostly obvious to others around them but, by definition, it can be very hard to spot in yourself.

We can all be short-sighted about our own behaviour and the impact of it, particularly if our own emotions or personal issues come into play. This is why you should spend time reflecting on your work practice and your interactions with clients. It is also the reason why social care workers need good line management, clinical supervision where possible, and good support and feedback from colleagues.

Having a good clear understanding of your own issues, personality, needs and working style and how this can impact on others is the best way to avoid and spot subconscious boundary crossings (see Chapter 11, 'Self-awareness', for more information). You can also use the list of warning signs of boundary crossings below to help you analyse your work and your actions.

One simple question

One very simple question you can ask yourself is: 'How comfortable would I feel explaining this entire situation to my boss and the rest of my team in full unedited detail?

If you would feel uncomfortable, or would feel the need to edit some of what happened. then a boundary has probably been crossed.

WARNING SIGNS OF BROKEN BOUNDARIES

The situations listed below are all possible warning signs that you are breaking boundaries, or are in danger of breaking boundaries. It does not necessarily mean that there is a problem, but any of these signs should, at the very least, make you stop and think. These signs will help you spot that emotional boundaries have been crossed by you or the client and will help you spot your subconscious boundary crossings:

- *Thinking or talking about clients when away from work.* Taking your work home with you is inevitable to a certain extent. However, if you are keeping your boundaries with your clients and managing your own emotions, this should not happen too often. If you find yourself thinking about particular clients on a regular basis you should think closely about your emotional links with the client and why you are so focused on them.

- *Prioritising a particular client.* If you have a client with high support needs it can be difficult to judge how much time to allocate to them. However, if the needs/demands of one client consistently take up a high proportion of your time then you should think carefully about why you are prioritising this client in particular.

- *Sessions regularly over-running.* If you are regularly over-running the allotted time with a client there may well be some dependence or co-dependence between you that is leading you to break simple time boundaries.

- *Sessions regularly finishing early.* If on the other hand your sessions are finishing early then one of you is avoiding something or is sabotaging the relationship. There may well be some mirroring of behaviour going on as you pick up each other's issues.

- *Spending free time at work, socialising with a client.* If you find yourself chatting socially with a particular client on a regular basis, if you seek each other out for a chat, or if your relationship is becoming more and more sociable you should keep a close eye on the dynamics of your relationship.

- *Sharing personal information with a client.* If you find yourself sharing more personal information than strictly necessary with a client, particularly if you are volunteering the information, then you need to ask yourself why.

- *Sharing worries about work with a client.* If you are talking to the client about problems or difficulties of work that don't relate to them, either having a moan or offloading your feelings, then you are starting to treat them like a colleague and putting your needs first.

- *Feeling responsible, guilty or down when a client does not progress.* If you are taking personal responsibility for a client's life/lifestyle/progress then either you are becoming overly attached and involved, or you have not been doing your job to the best of your ability and are feeling guilty as a result.

- *Increased physical touching when interacting with a client.* Even if there are no sexual overtones to the physical contact, this is a clear sign that the relationship is moving into areas that it should not.

- *Unnecessary sexual content in conversations with a client.* Again another clear sign that the relationship is drifting away from being purely professional.

- *Keeping secrets with a client.* If you are sharing some private information, even if it is about something innocuous, then your relationship is heading into more personal territory.

- *Keeping secrets about a client.* If you are withholding relevant information, that would normally be disclosed, about a client from your team members or other professionals you are not only breaching standard good practice but it is a strong indication that you are over-involved with the client.

- *Being defensive if questioned about a client.* If you find yourself acting defensively when questioned about a client you are either becoming personally involved with the client's case and are defending the client, or are worried about your interactions or work with the client.

- *Finding it difficult to hand a client over to other services or workers (feeling possessive).* This is a clear indication that you have bonded a little too closely with the client and that they may be dependent on you, or you are dependent on your relationship with them.

- *Wishing that you had met in different circumstances.* If you feel that it is unfortunate that you had met as worker and client, not in a social situation so that you could be friends/lovers/business partners, then you have clearly become too attached to the client.

- *Dressing up when working with a particular client.* If you find yourself dressing more smartly, more relaxed, or attractively for a particular client then you are clearly too attached to what the client thinks of you. It may be an attraction between you or you may be focusing too much on your needs and how you are seen.

- *Treating a client differently from other clients.* If in any way your client is getting 'special' treatment you should closely examine why. If it is motivated by a clear assessment of client need and you would treat any other client with a similar need the same, then it may be justified. However, it may be that you are making allowances for a client unnecessarily, based on your personal feelings or needs.

- *Feeling strong emotion when you see a client.* Whether it is happiness, stress, sadness, depression, anxiety or joy, if a client is provoking strong feelings in you, you have crossed an emotional boundary and become too involved.

- *Other workers challenging you on your boundaries.* It is quite rare for a worker to challenge another worker on their work practice, so if it happens to you then you should sit up and take serious notice. Often your colleague may not have the full picture and their idea of the situation and the solution may not be correct. However, if they think you are crossing boundaries then you almost certainly are. Spend some time thinking about what these might be and how you can change your behaviour.

- *'Only you.'* If a client is telling you that only you understand them and no one else really gets them, they don't trust any other workers, or that you are special in some way, the alarm bells should start ringing. If this escalates into refusing to work with other workers then there is clearly an over-dependence on you.

- *Changes in behaviour.* If a client starts to push or crosses minor boundaries on a regular basis when they did not do so previously, it may well be a sign of an emotional boundary having shifted.

- *Physical contact.* If a client is holding your hand for slightly too long when you shake their hand, keeps putting their arm around your shoulder, touching you when they talk, not only are they stepping over the physical touch boundary but this may well be a sign of a crossed emotional boundary.

- *Hanging around.* If a client is often hanging around when you are on shift, or waiting for you as you come out of a session with another client, or outside the building when you leave, they are probably becoming too dependent on you.

- *Eye contact.* Eye contact can be interpreted in many different ways, but we are all able to read the eyes of people around us. If the way your client uses eye contact differs around you there may be something going on for them regarding the relationship.

- *Nicknames.* If a client starts to call you by a nickname of any sort they may be starting to get over-familiar. Some people do it to everyone, which makes it less personal and less serious. If the nickname is personalised and the client does not usually use nicknames then you should challenge the behaviour and get them to use your normal name.

- *Flirting.* Flirting is obviously boundary crossing behaviour and of course it could be a sign of attraction or of manipulation.

- *Compliments.* If a client is being very nice to you and very complimentary on a regular basis this may also be a sign that they are looking at the relationship in an inappropriate way.

- *Unjustified complaints.* If a client is making what turn out to be unjustified complaints about a worker, it can be a sign that a boundary has been crossed but the client cannot correctly identify what it is, or that an emotional boundary has been crossed, causing the client to complain about other issues.

- *Pushing time boundaries.* If a client is pushing for extra time or extra sessions, or always brings up a big issue as the session is about to end, they may be becoming too dependent on you.

2. Analysis

Once you have spotted that a boundary has been crossed you need to get an idea of how serious it is and what the potential harm may be so that you can make a judgement of what to do. However, you do not need to come to an exact conclusion about where on the scale an action is. A rough idea of the seriousness of the incident will do.

There are three different areas that you need to look at to get a full picture of the incident:

- What happened?
- The background to the incident.
- The potential harm caused by the incident.

WHAT HAPPENED?

The first thing we need to understand is the basic events that constitute the potential boundary crossing. What was done, who did it, where and when was it done? Even these basic facts can change the way you think about a situation. Look at the list of situations below, all of which refer to a worker and client hugging.

A simple description such as 'a worker and client hugged' does not give you enough information to make any kind of judgement. This list gives you an idea of the range of situations that could be covered:

- The client unexpectedly and suddenly hugs the worker, but the worker does not return the hug, keeps body contact to a minimum and gets out of the hug as soon as possible.

- The client unexpectedly and suddenly hugs the worker and the worker returns the hug briefly then disengages.

- The client offers a hug to the worker and the worker accepts the hug briefly.

- The worker puts their arm around the client's shoulders when they are upset.

- The client offers a hug to the worker and gets a good hug in return.

- The client offers to hug the worker and the worker embraces the client tightly and lifts them off the ground.

- The worker offers a hug to the client.

- The worker suddenly and unexpectedly hugs the client.

- The worker offers a hug to the client and pats them gently on the back reassuringly.

- The worker offers the client a hug and clasps tight, their entire bodies pressing tightly together.

- The worker asks the client for a hug and then buries his head in her neck and weeps and sobs.

Even a brief analysis of these incidents shows that there are many grades of boundary crossing with even a simple incident like a hug.

The first incident is boundaried behaviour from the worker, but a boundary has been crossed by the client. The last two incidents are well over the line of acceptable behaviour from the worker. The rest of the incidents are clearly at the very least inappropriate and possibly gross misconduct, but the seriousness of the crossing varies massively.

You can also see that you cannot really judge the issue without further detail and background to the situation.

BACKGROUND

The information about what happened on its own is not enough to make any kind of judgement. To get a full picture of all the implications, and seriousness of the situation, we also have to take into account the background to the situation:

- *The client's personal background.* What is the client's gender and age, their personal experience and any issues that they suffer from, are they a vulnerable adult or child, how do they normally behave and what is their history of interactions with other staff?

- *The role of the worker.* How intimate, in-depth or personal is the service the worker provides for the client? What is normal for a worker in this role?

- *The context.* What led up to the action or situation? What were the surrounding issues?

- *History of the relationship.* Have there been previous similar boundary crossings? How long have they been working together and what is the pre-existing dynamic between the worker and the client?

All of these factors need to be considered when judging how serious the situation is.

POTENTIAL HARM

For the final piece of the jigsaw we need to look at the potential harm that could be caused by the incident. Essentially this is a risk assessment exercise and so fits into the standard risk model of assessing the *magnitude* of the harm and the *probability* of the harm.

The judgement of the magnitude and probability of harm will be based on our knowledge of what happened and the background.

We have to look at the potential harm rather than the actual harm caused. Since you cannot tell at the time of the incident/action the full extent of the harm, you have to judge the incident for its potential.

It is true that occasionally a serious boundary crossing may not cause too much harm and, conversely, a minor boundary crossing can cause a disproportionate amount of harm. However, this fact can never be used to justify actions retrospectively. Given that we are supposed to be responsible professionals safeguarding our clients' welfare, we should not be taking unnecessary risks.

Analysis case studies

Let us use the example of a client and worker hugging to illustrate how complex the situation can be. Clearly workers and clients are not supposed to hug, and so, on the surface, it is quite a simple matter. However, as we delve into each area the complexity emerges. Here are two case studies to demonstrate some of the factors at work.

Case Study 1
WHAT HAPPENED?
The worker offers the client a hug and clasps tight, their entire bodies pressing tightly together.

BACKGROUND

- *The client's personal background*: a young woman with a history of being sexually abused.

- *The role of the worker*: one-to-one psychodynamic counsellor.

- *Where the hug took place*: in a private therapy room.

- *The context*: the client has been telling the worker how lonely and unloved they feel.

- *History of the relationship*: the client has shown signs of being attracted to the worker.

In this situation we would judge the worker quite harshly for hugging the client. The client is obviously vulnerable (although not necessarily a 'vulnerable adult'), the relationship is in-depth and intimate, the hug was private and therefore more personal, giving a hug directly feeds into the client's issues that they were discussing at the time and there are previous factors that should have warned the worker to be careful about physical contact.

POTENTIAL HARM

- Client believes that the worker is attracted to her and reciprocates.

- Client feels violated and abused by the invasion of her personal space by a trusted support worker, bringing up and reinforcing previous negative feelings.

- Client feels safe and protected and becomes overly dependent on the worker.

- Client accuses the worker of abusing her.

- Client does not attend further sessions.

- Client loses trust in support workers/counsellors generally.

- Worker's integrity is compromised and client can manipulate the worker.

- Client tells other clients about what happened and the worker's/organisation's reputation is damaged.

RISK ASSESSMENT

The harm here is maximised because the hug was intimate, in private and initiated by the worker, the relationship was in-depth and requires great trust.

Given the number of background issues highlighting the vulnerability of the client and the impact that it may have on her, we would judge that there is a high risk of serious consequences.

Case Study 2
WHAT HAPPENED?

The client unexpectedly and suddenly hugs the worker and the worker returns the hug briefly then disengages.

BACKGROUND

- *The client's personal background*: a stable young woman who had lost her job.
- *The role of the worker*: a support worker at a job club.
- *Where the hug took place*: in the reception area of the project.
- *The context*: the client had just got a job.
- *History of the relationship*: the client has focused on finding a job, worked hard and engaged well.

We would then judge the situation less harshly, although boundaries have still been crossed. There are no obvious warning signs in the background, the relationship is not very in-depth or personal, it is an obvious context for a congratulatory hug and the background did not present any obvious issues.

POTENTIAL HARM

- Other clients see the hug and think it is normal to hug workers.
- Other clients believe that there is a 'special relationship' and that is why the client got a job.
- The client believes the worker is attracted to her.

RISK ASSESSMENT

The harm is minimised because the hug was initiated by the client, the worker–client relationship is about to end and they did not have an in-depth relationship.

The chance of the harm occurring is probably medium but the seriousness of the harm is probably low.

Neither of the lists of possible harm in the case studies above are exhaustive, but they represent a range of possible outcomes. It is always possible that the client in Case Study 1 would not pay much attention to the hug and just take it as a sympathetic gesture and that the client in Case Study 2 may be more traumatised than we would imagine and makes a complaint.

It is never possible to anticipate every possible outcome, but you can foresee the likely outcomes and work to avoid them. At the end of the day the more you look after your basic boundaries, the less often you will find yourself in a situation where you are assessing possible harm.

3. Action

A minor broken boundary if left unchecked could develop into a much more serious issue. If dealt with appropriately and quickly then it may remain a minor matter.

Once you have spotted and analysed a boundary crossing situation you must take some action to re-set the boundaries and try to offset any damage. Even a minor boundary crossing needs to be addressed in some way, even if it is just by becoming more vigilant. As well as any actions suggested below you need to use your skills as a worker and your relationship with the client to manage the issue as sensitively as possible back onto safe ground.

It may sometimes be unclear whether a boundary has been crossed or not. If you are unsure then treat it as if it has been crossed, but change the emphasis of your actions accordingly. So if you think that a client has crossed an emotional boundary you could discuss the issue of boundaries with them rather than suggest that they have crossed a boundary. It is better to take some action when in doubt, rather than letting a crossed boundary slip by unchecked. (For more information and ideas about dealing with crossed boundaries see Chapter 10, 'Maintaining Boundaries'.)

If any boundary is crossed you must at the very least take the following actions:

- *Make sure all your other boundaries are in place.* What other boundaries have not been in place that have led to this crossing? Have a thorough re-examination of your boundaries and make sure that, going forward, all of the basics are firmly in place.

- *Be alert/on your guard.* Effectively, once a boundary has been crossed you need to make sure that you are more aware than normal and take care to examine your actions and your client's actions more closely in the near future.

There is no magic wand to undo a crossed boundary but there are a number of other things that you can do. Most of them are fairly simple but they are effective if applied thoroughly. You need to use your judgement as to which of the following actions is appropriate/ necessary. The severity of the boundary crossing will influence the extent of your actions.

TAKE NOTES

If you take notes on your work with clients as a matter of course, then any boundary crossings should be recorded, even relatively small ones. This is particularly important if you see a pattern of boundary crossings. The notes will help you spot these patterns.

If a serious boundary crossing occurs, one that might at a later date involve the law, or questions of responsibility or professional accountability, then you should make careful notes about what happened as soon as you can, even if you don't normally take notes. This will enable you to have a clear and detailed record of events for any future inquiry.

TELL YOUR LINE MANAGER

If a boundary of any significance has been crossed then you should inform your line manager as soon as possible. The importance of this cannot be over-emphasised. Telling your line manager ensures that it does not look like you are hiding anything or colluding with a client. If your manager finds out that a boundary has been crossed and you have not told them about it, then it looks remarkably suspicious, particularly if the crossing comes to light whilst investigating other incidents or boundary crossings.

If the boundary has been crossed by the client, it can sometimes be useful to sit down and analyse the situation with someone who is not so closely involved. This enables you to discuss an appropriate course of action with the sanction of your manager. It also allows your manager to assess and understand any risks involved, either to you, other staff and clients or the organisation.

Speak to the client

With many boundary crossings it is worth talking to the client about the situation that has occurred and discussing the implications for them and/or you. Explain the situation to them assertively, acknowledge the factors involved and be honest. If you have made a mistake and crossed a boundary yourself, own the mistake and explain what you will do differently in the future. It may be a useful learning experience for the client.

This does not need to be done in every situation and you should use your judgement about the situation and the client in question to decide when it is appropriate.

Restate the boundaries

Very simply, if a boundary has been crossed, you need to remind whoever has crossed the boundary what the appropriate behaviour is and why they should not cross the boundary in future. Sometimes this is enough to prevent a further occurrence. Even if it does not prevent future crossings, you still need to ensure that the client knows and understands what they are doing wrong.

It can be useful to get a more senior worker to explain the boundaries and lay down the law a bit with the client. This does, however, come with the danger of disempowering the worker.

Offset the harm

This really depends on the exact nature of the boundary crossing and often telling your manager and colleagues and talking to the client may be all you can do. However, there are situations where there is further action you can take. New ways of working with the client can be introduced, outside agencies can be informed about what has happened, the client or anyone else affected could be offered extra support, or a meeting could be held with the rest of the client group to explain what has happened or to reinforce boundaries in this area.

Tell colleagues

You should speak to your colleagues about boundary crossings for a number of reasons. They may have spotted similar behaviour and your information may give them a fuller picture. They will know to be aware around a particular client or when dealing with a particular situation. Other staff being aware means that they can work to prevent further boundary crossings occurring.

Deal with the root cause

Crossed boundaries are usually a symptom of something else, so it is important that you pick up on what is going on for the individual who has crossed a boundary. You will usually find that there is a support issue there for the client or the worker – often an emotion or an unmet need is at the root of the boundary crossing.

A client may be lonely and needs to build up more friends, or is angry and scared about another issue. A worker may be frustrated or stuck with a client or have insufficient training. Whatever the issue is, you need to spend some time supporting the client or getting support for yourself around this issue. This may be a longer process and may involve other skills and techniques or a referral to other workers or services.

Refocus support plan/care plan

If you have identified a serious boundary crossing such as a client becoming overly dependent on you, you need to incorporate dealing with the issue into your support/care plan for the client.

End the relationship

In more serious cases, particularly if the worker feels unsafe working with the client, or it does not seem possible to set the relationship back on an appropriate footing, it may be necessary to change workers. This should be done as carefully and as sensitively as possible. The client and worker may have built up a strong relationship and suddenly ending the relationship with no warning could be unhelpful. Having a crossover period and three-way meetings can help ease the transition. Of course, in serious cases this may not be possible.

Consequences

If the crossed boundary is as a result of client action then you need to decide if there are any consequences for the client. An action would need to be quite inappropriate for there to be a serious consequence. In most cases you should give someone a clear warning on at least one occasion (if not more) before taking any serious measures. Depending on the setting you work in and the client group, this may be more or less feasible. Consequences need to be fair, reasonable and appropriate to the seriousness of the crossing.

BEHAVIOUR CONTRACTS

Another way to work with a client when they have crossed a boundary/boundaries is to draw up a specific behaviour contract with that client. The contract lays out clearly what behaviour is or is not expected from the client and what the consequences will be if they breach the contract. It is then signed by both worker and client. This enables you to continue to work with the client in the short term, but does mean that their behaviour is not going unchecked.

Treading a fine line

Worker: John, working as a learning mentor

Client: Beth, now living in her own flat after four years of sleeping rough and two years in temporary housing/hostels

John has been supporting Beth in going to college by helping her deal with emotional and practical issues that come up. They meet once a week at his office and Beth has been engaging well and working really hard and using his services well.

Towards the end of her course there is an awards ceremony and Beth asks John to attend the ceremony. He arrives at the college early and so they get a coffee and sit around chatting. Beth and John start talking about books that they have read and find that they have both read and enjoyed *The Da Vinci Code*. They talk about the book and have an interesting and enjoyable discussion about religion and myths.

When it is time to go to the ceremony Beth says how much she has enjoyed talking to John about literature. She doesn't get a chance to talk to anyone about this sort of stuff these days and she really misses it.

Next time John sees her she brings in another book by the same author and offers to lend it to him and asks if he has any good books to read because she has run out and is desperate for some more good reads. He refuses and says it is outside his boundaries.

The time after that she asks if he fancies going out for a coffee to talk about a TV show they both watched. He refuses again.

Later that week she calls him up for a chat out of hours.

- Identify any boundaries that have been crossed.

- What should John have done differently?

- When should he have been alerted that something was wrong?

- What action can he take now?

Should he shop him?

Worker: Junior, a volunteer at a day centre for rough sleepers

Client: Lee, a rough sleeper who accesses the day centre

Junior goes with Lee to his local post office to help him set up an account to start receiving benefits. Lee is a heavy drinker and normally ends up shouting and leaving when trying to get anything official done.

Whilst in the post office Lee makes a big fuss in front of the cashier and the queue about how much Junior is helping him and how wonderful he is. The cashier says that it is great that people like him are helping others and that if he has any other clients that need help with benefits he is happy to do what he can.

When they get back to the day centre, Lee pulls a sandwich out from his pocket and starts to eat it. It is a sandwich from the post office (which is part of a larger shop). Junior knows he did not buy it.

- Identify any boundaries that have been crossed.

- What should Junior have done differently?

- When should he have been alerted that something was wrong?

- What action can he take now?

Chapter 9

Understanding Negative Consequences

There are a host of problems that can be caused by stepping over your boundaries or not managing your client's boundary crossings. This chapter covers some of the most common. You will notice that each negative consequence can cause other negative consequences and the pushing of more boundaries. In this way a snowball effect can occur with a relationship becoming more out of control, less focused and more inappropriate if it is not dealt with.

Unrealistic expectations

Unboundaried behaviour can often lead to the client having expectations that the worker cannot meet. If you step outside the boundaries by giving your client extra time in a session, they may come to expect that treatment as standard. When you are unable to continue they can become resentful. This affects the work that you are doing and ultimately the client loses out.

If you start to develop role confusion and the client starts to see you as a friend or in a parental role they will start to expect treatment that you as a worker cannot deliver. Again this can set up a difficult and unhealthy dynamic in the relationship.

Workers who get too emotionally involved with their clients are prone to start making promises to help the client achieve something that may be unrealistic. A worker may promise access to further services or housing, for example, believing that they will be able to pull a few strings and sort it out for the client. If it is not possible to achieve what is promised the relationship suffers, or the worker is drawn into colluding with the client that the system is unfair, or some other belief used to justify the situation.

This can also cause problems within a team. If one worker has loose boundaries, clients start to expect to be treated loosely, so that when they encounter a boundaried worker there is tension as a result.

Clients withdrawing

If the way you work does not make people feel safe or that they can trust you, then clients are more likely to withdraw from the service. It takes an unusually brave and confident client to confront a worker about such issues. Vulnerable clients with low self-esteem are much more likely to isolate from the service and just not engage. It can be very hard for clients to feel strong enough to reach out and ask for support – a bad experience can really set them back and do further damage to an already fragile individual.

Damage to clients

Overstepping your boundaries can easily breach the trust that the client has placed in you. Not only will it damage their chances of getting the help that they really need, but it can impact very negatively on their psyche.

Even if what has happened would not be termed abuse in the traditional sense, if you have breached trust then you are in an abusive relationship. Abusive relationships can cause feelings of humiliation, shame, guilt, low self-esteem, depression, loss of confidence and a wide range of other negative impacts.

Resentment/anger

Poorly managed boundaries can lead to resentment by the client you are working with if they feel that they are getting a raw deal, or from other clients if they feel that you are not dealing with them all fairly and consistently. Resentment can spill out in many different ways, and clearly none of them are useful for the process of engaging with social care services.

Appearance of impropriety

If you have been breaking boundaries and working in inappropriate ways with a client it can appear to others that what is happening is more sinister than it really is. If a problem occurs or an accusation is made you can end up in a position that is very hard to justify or defend.

This is particularly difficult in the case of false accusations, and if you are working in an unboundaried way there is a much greater chance of false accusations. Because your clients, other clients and workers are likely to become resentful of your behaviour, there is a much greater chance of someone complaining about you.

Once an investigation is started, even if the accusation or suspicion is entirely untrue, if your work practice is full of broken boundaries it will be much harder to clear your name. What may have been seen by the client as a favour, or extra help, can come back to haunt you.

Taking gifts – or taking advantage?

Worker: John, a site manager in a supported housing project for elderly residents

Client: Liz, an elderly resident whose few remaining family members do not visit often

John has 50 residents on the estate to support. He works from nine until five and lives on the estate. Residents can contact him in an emergency outside his working hours. His role is to keep an eye on things and deal with the maintenance of the estate. He is not supposed to get involved with the day-to-day care of the residents.

Liz and John get on very well as they grew up in the same part of the country. He often pops in at the end of the day for a cup of tea and a chat as he knows that she is lonely. They often sit and admire a lovely painting of their local area and reminisce; the painting is of some fields that John used to play in when he was a child. The other residents are jealous that Liz gets so much attention.

Liz breaks her hip one day and it leaves her housebound and very inactive. John does some shopping for her, picks up some prescriptions for her and fits a new shelf next to her bed so that she can keep things in easy reach. As she recovers, Liz says she is so grateful for the help he has given her that she wants to give him the painting as thanks. He protests but she insists.

Feeling obligated because of the picture, John continues to support Liz above and beyond his normal duties. The other residents are suspicious when one of them notices the painting hanging in his house.

A few months later it is discovered that Liz has a very aggressive and terminal disease and she dies shortly afterwards. At the reading of her will it is discovered that she has left a large chunk of her £100,000 savings to John. Her family are very angry and accuse John of conning her out of the money and taking advantage of her. When they hear that the extremely valuable painting that was a family heirloom was in his house months before she died, they make an official complaint.

John's manager does an initial investigation and finds that John was working outside of his role, outside of his hours and hears lots of complaints from the other residents.

Dependency

If a client becomes too dependent on a particular worker they are more likely to become disempowered over the long term and may also suffer if for some reason they are unable to see the worker.

If you are working with a dependent client, it is very hard work, draining, and your work may falter with the client falling back into old patterns of behaviour despite much hard work on both parts. Ultimately by allowing or encouraging a client to become dependent on you, you are setting them up to fail.

There are very few social care roles where motivation and empowerment are not key to the aims of the service/relationship. Most services will be supporting clients to make or manage some kind of change. True change is something that other people do, it is not something that we can do for them.

You can support clients and help them change, but motivation comes from within. Becoming dependent will reinforce the subconscious message that the client cannot do things for themself, which is ultimately self-defeating. Even if dependent clients move forward with their issues or make positive changes, if they are unable to sustain these changes after the end of the relationship then the work will have been wasted.

Some level of dependency is natural within the relationship and with some clients is bound to occur. This means that you have to be even more aware and manage dependency issues even more closely.

It is worth bearing in mind that even if you have a long time to work with a client there can be changes outside of your control that may impact on the relationship. Funding changes, long-term sickness, accidents or job offers can all end a relationship abruptly. You should try to keep your relationship with clients in a state that means that they can withstand such changes without too much impact on their lives and their support needs.

Transference

Transference is a concept first described by Sigmund Freud and is a very important tool for psychoanalysts. Most social care workers won't use it in this way, but it is important to be aware of it. The concept is commonly understood by most people but can be hard to spot in practice.

Transference occurs when someone projects feelings about important people in their life onto a current relationship. Quite often they will be feelings about parents, but they can be other significant people from their past. If a client is angry at their father for example, then they may become angry if their worker reminds them of their father. This can happen to anyone with any other person. However, the role of a social care worker is similar to many aspects of being a parent, so we need to be extra careful.

The more information someone has about you, particularly personal information, the greater chance there is that they will project onto you their feelings about someone from their past.

Attachment

Attachment is another psychoanalytic idea that has entered the public consciousness. This is when someone has an unmet need from a previous relationship and they try to get that need met in a new relationship. If for example a client had a very unforgiving and judgemental mother then they might become very attached to any female worker who is non-judgemental and forgiving. Many of us have complex relationships with our parents, and clients in many social care settings are more likely to have had a difficult or troubled relationship. A good social care professional will provide a safe and positive relationship for the client. Unfortunately, this is more likely to trigger off attachment problems for clients who have had negative parental experiences.

Once a client becomes overly attached they are more likely to become dependent, unfocused, have unrealistic expectations and they will start to push other boundaries. This will cause tension within the relationship and pressure on the worker.

Distraction from task/purpose

Whatever your job, you will have certain goals that you are aiming towards. If you let your client's whims, confusion or multiple needs drag you around from pillar to post, you will find that your original aims get lost.

Clients may be very happy just having someone to talk to once a week without doing much actual work – just giving them a massage rather than working specifically on their bad hip. However, your role is to provide some professional focus and detachment.

If you become emotionally involved, if managing boundaries becomes so complex that you don't get any work done, if you let your client dictate everything about your time together, you may well end up not achieving much.

Even the most basic boundaries such as timekeeping, note-taking and structure will keep you focused on the task that you are doing and stop sessions becoming social time.

Splitting a team

When working as a team you need to keep your boundaries as in line with each other's as possible. It is not possible to match each other exactly, but if there are glaring differences then problems will start to occur.

If there is not enough communication and trust within the team, then loose boundaries can be exploited by the clients. This can start to build resentment and frustration within the team and will cause other boundaries to be broken:

'Jim always lets us do it…'

'Maureen said it's ok…'

'Billy promised me that I would be accepted.'

These are all common statements to hear from clients in a project. Either the other workers have been slack with their boundaries, or the clients are trying to test the boundaries or have misheard what was originally said.

These comments need to be met with a boundaried response. It is important that you don't undermine the previous worker with your response, but neither should you allow clients to overstep boundaries or manipulate you. If the worker in question does not have enough information, or does not have enough trust in the other worker's boundaries, then it will be very hard to deal with the situation.

Manipulation

Clients who have been 'in the system' for a while will have a good understanding of how workers should and should not behave. If you break boundaries, this can be used to manipulate you in a variety of ways. Outright blackmail is not common, but can happen. The more boundaries you cross the more vulnerable you make yourself.

Disciplinary action

Stepping outside of your boundaries and not managing your work and your relationships properly can lead to disciplinary action from your employer. This has obvious and clear difficulties for you as a worker, but also causes great problems for the clients who you are working with. If you are suspended from work whilst an investigation goes on, even if you are cleared of any wrongdoing, your clients will suffer, as will your career.

Barring

At the extreme end of disciplinary action is the possibility that you may get barred from working in your particular profession or from working with vulnerable people. With new safeguarding legislation and barring and vetting schemes you could effectively end your career in social care. If you are working with vulnerable adults you need to be particularly vigilant. It is easy to let bad habits slip into neglect without any intention to do so.

Lack of protection

Working in social care is a very responsible job: vulnerable people rely on you for support and you are expected to measure up. Sadly, despite our best efforts, things do go wrong, in the system and/or in the lives of our clients.

Your employers, professional bodies, funders, law courts and tribunals will all expect you to behave within your professional boundaries. If a serious incident or accident occurs involving one of your clients it could end up with a compensation claim, tribunal, serious case review, disciplinary hearing or court case.

Your behaviour and working practices will come under a great deal of scrutiny. If you have not abided by your professional boundaries it will be looked at very critically. In the busy day-to-day rush of a job, you may be able to justify letting things slip and not doing things properly, but in the cold light of an investigation it will look very different.

If you have abided by policy and procedure and done everything by the book, then, for the most part, you will be protected by the law, any professional bodies you are a member of and the organisation that you work for. If you have stepped outside your boundaries then the full responsibility for your actions will fall upon you.

Abuse

There are a few predatory individuals who will seek out vulnerable clients with the express purpose of abusing them. However, many cases of abuse by social care professionals happen as part of a slide from boundaried behaviour into more and more inappropriate behaviour. You may think that it would not or could not happen to you, but if you let enough boundaries slide, things can get out of control.

If you are working with vulnerable adults and children then the scope of what counts as abuse is much broader. Given we have a duty of care over our clients and neglect is a major form of abuse, you must be very careful that poor work practices do not lead you inadvertently into an abusive situation.

Don't be fooled into thinking that because a client is complicit and happy to do something then it does not count as abuse. Even if a client initiates an action, is in full control of what they do and is not forced to do anything, it can be classed as abuse. Clients may not be aware of, or may not care, what is appropriate behaviour. As the professional, you are responsible for what happens in the relationship.

Serious abuse of an individual, particularly by an individual in a position of trust, has long-term and far-reaching impacts on that client that may be with them for the rest of their life.

Chapter 10

Maintaining Boundaries

There are many skills and techniques that you will need to use to maintain and manage your boundaries and those of your clients. This chapter contains a few key techniques and pieces of information to help you.

Making a boundaries decision

Some boundary crossings occur and then you have to deal with them. However, there are often times when you have to make a decision on a course of action and you need to decide if a given course of action is within your boundaries or outside your boundaries. There is unfortunately no golden rule, but a list of factors that you need to consider includes:

- What are the client's needs?
- Are there any rules or policies relevant to this decision?
- What is my role, and am I within my role in taking this action?
- What are the client's motivations?
- How would other members of staff deal with this situation?
- What impact will my decision have on other members of staff?
- What impact will my decision have on other clients?
- What impact will my decision have on this client's life?
- What impact will this decision have on my relationship with this client?

- What are my conscious/subconscious motivations?
- Are my needs getting in the way of the correct decision?

High-risk situations

As the name implies, a high-risk situation is one in which there is a higher than normal risk of boundaries being crossed by either you or the client. Once you have identified that you are in a high-risk situation you need to be alert for the possibility of other boundaries being broken.

You must have a quick boundaries check-up with yourself, ensure that you are ultra-rigorous with all your basic boundaries. Ideally have a chat with another member of staff, line manager or supervisor about the situation and how to manage it.

Not all of the following situations will apply to everyone; different people have different triggers and different high-risk situations. You may well identify other high-risk situations that are particular to you that are not on this list.

Identifying with clients' issues

If a client's experience or personality matches with your own on any level then there is an increased chance that you will break some boundaries. This is because you are more likely to bond on a personal level, because your own issues and feelings will interfere with your judgement, or they will pick up on the link between you.

Strong feelings

Often a client, or a client's story, will evoke strong feelings in you. Maybe you feel sorry for them, angry with what they have to say, feel sad and want to cry. Whatever the feeling may be, strong emotions will open you up and make you more vulnerable to your own impulses and less focused on boundary keeping.

Personal issues

If you are going through any major issues outside of work they can leave you drained, tired and unfocused. You will be less focused on someone else's needs and are more likely to be less thorough and may miss something you would normally pick up on.

Tired/stressed

As with personal issues, if you are very tired or stressed you are more likely to cross boundaries yourself or to let a situation develop where boundaries will be crossed. In addition, if you are stressed you need to make sure that your stress is being managed and dealt with outside of your client sessions and that you do not end up taking it out on them.

Overworked

If your caseload or workload is too high, not only will you be tired and stressed but you may not have adequate time to refresh and focus yourself before sessions with clients, or to write up notes and do any additional work in between sessions.

Frustrating/difficult clients

If you are finding it hard to work with a client, if they are hard to engage, manipulative or their emotional issues make it hard to work with them, you may end up crossing boundaries in order to get the relationship to 'work'. It is after all your job to engage them, and so whilst trying different methods to reach out to them you may go a step too far. Your growing frustration may also lead you to cross boundaries.

Likeable clients

Whilst easy to work with, likeable clients will generally be less likely to break minor boundaries. However, this can lull you into a false sense of security. If you relax too much and assume everything will be easy you may drift into a situation where you or they may cross a boundary more easily.

Attractive clients

If you find yourself sexually attracted to a client, there is a very high risk of boundaries being crossed. As a professional it should not be too hard to avoid flirting with them or anything more serious happening. Even then, however, your attention will be distracted by managing this situation, your ego and your insecurities are more likely to come into play and you will be more open to being manipulated by the client.

The attraction creates an extra dynamic for you to have to manage for yourself and the distraction may lead to other unrelated boundaries being broken. If you do find that the attraction is really distracting from the work you are doing, maybe another worker should work with the client.

Manipulative clients

If you have a client who is obviously trying to manipulate you in some way then ensure that all your boundaries are managed tightly. If you leave a chink in your boundaries armour, they will find a way to exploit it. Of course, a good manipulator is not obvious about it so keep alert. An obvious 'tell' for a manipulative client is that they are very self-centred and can be very changeable in mood, from very friendly to aggressive and back again.

Accidental meeting

Whilst you are at work, you will be focused and prepared and be in 'work mode', which helps with managing boundaries. If you bump into a client outside of work, you are unprepared and unfocused and it is much easier to slip up and cross a boundary. This is particularly so if you bump into a client whilst you are socialising and have been drinking.

Non-standard work environment

If you are with a client in an environment that is different from your normal working environment you will be more likely to let boundaries slip. We all have a certain chameleon-like quality and adapt to our surroundings. Sitting in a café is a much more relaxed situation than in your place of work; sitting on a sofa in someone's house is a much more personal situation than in your place of work. You will not have your normal cues to keep you in your professional space and you are more likely to relax.

If you regularly do home visits or work with clients in other non-traditional work environments then client's homes will become a standard work environment and will not be high risk.

Down time

If you are doing an assessment, delivering a key work session, facilitating a group, giving a treatment or are in any other formal work setting, it is much easier to maintain and manage your boundaries. If, however, you are on reception duty and a client is hanging around chatting or if you are travelling somewhere together it is a bit more difficult. It is much easier to cross boundaries or let them be crossed when you are casually chatting with clients, or spending an unfocused period of time with them.

If a boundary has been crossed

As soon as one boundary has been crossed, for any reason, by you or the client, you are in a high-risk situation. Other boundary crossings are more likely to follow as a direct result of the first crossing because one boundary crossing is often a sign of other issues surfacing, issues that may well surface again shortly.

If you notice signs of attachment/dependence

Once you notice any signs of attachment, dependence or any other inappropriate relationship from the client (or yourself), you should be on high alert. Clearly the relationship is heading in the wrong direction and boundary crossings will surely follow.

Starting a new job

Starting a new job always takes a lot of effort and concentration. There is a danger that whilst you concentrate on new procedures, different assessment forms and other new ways of working then you forget your boundaries.

Being assertive

The key skill required for maintaining boundaries is assertiveness. It is very obvious and the concept is simple, but not everyone can get the balance right.

You can understand all the key concepts of professional boundaries, but if you do not have good enough personal confidence and communication skills you will not be able to put them into action effectively on the ground.

You have to be able to challenge clients on their words or actions, enforce rules, deal with manipulative behaviour, stand your ground under pressure, all with a smile on your face whilst listening sympathetically. To do all this and still maintain a good relationship with your clients is a challenge.

In essence, being assertive is about getting a balance between being passive and aggressive. Someone who is assertive will confidently put forward their position or viewpoint whilst respecting other people's rights and feelings.

How assertive/passive/aggressive you are depends on how much you respect other people's personal boundaries and how much you defend your own boundaries. Someone who is passive can be easily manipulated or abused because they don't hold their ground and stand up for themselves. Someone who is aggressive will bully and dominate others and ignore other people's feelings.

We will all have a particular way of managing our own personal boundaries and we may be assertive in some situations and passive in others. However you manage your boundaries outside of work, you need to be as assertive as possible whilst working with clients.

Dealing with boundary crossings or difficult boundary situations may require you to have conversations that both you and the client find uncomfortable territory. To be able to say what it is you mean, clearly and in a way that the client can accept, requires assertiveness.

If you manage boundaries too rigidly, tightly or aggressively then you will not be able to build the required bond with the clients. If on the other hand you are unable to manage your personal boundaries and let clients walk all over you and manipulate you, you will have no control and little respect.

If you have trouble with asserting yourself then you should consider getting some training, talk about it in supervision, attend some workshops or do some personal therapy.

How to communicate assertively

Assertive communication requires you to listen to what is being said as well as communicating clearly:

- Be totally honest about what you are trying to say, and in particular what you feel.

- Use a firm but not aggressive tone of voice, keep the volume steady and no louder than necessary.

- Be clear about what it is that you want. Don't skirt round the issue: 'I would really like you all to tidy up the communal lounge more often,' rather than, 'It's very messy in here.'

- Make relaxed but steady eye contact without staring them out.

- Make sure your body language is confident but relaxed. Stand tall but relaxed; relax your shoulders. Don't tell someone what you want whilst staring at your feet.

- Acknowledge what the other person has said and let them know that you have heard it: 'So you're tired after you come back from college and don't feel like doing anything. I appreciate it's difficult for you but I would really appreciate it if you could find some time to do it.'

- Ask open-ended questions that don't contain the answer: 'What other times could you do some tidying up,' rather than, 'Can't you just do it on Saturday morning?'

- Keep to the facts of a matter, don't exaggerate or use absolute words (never, always, everyone, only): 'The living room has only been cleaned once in the last month and the hoovering was last done two weeks ago,' rather than, 'This place is never cleaned, it's always totally disgusting and only I ever do the hoovering.'

- If you are going to criticise what someone has done, be specific about what is wrong rather than judgemental: 'The cleaning was done but the TV was not dusted and the windows were not cleaned,' rather than, 'That was an awful bit of cleaning. Didn't you learn anything at home?'

- Make sure that you use the word 'I' wherever possible to own the feelings you have: 'I find it really frustrating when the place is so dirty and I have worked hard to try and keep it clean,' rather than, 'We all hate it when it's dirty, anyone would be annoyed.'

Explaining boundaries

An incredibly common response by a worker to a request or question from a client is: 'Sorry, I can't do that because of professional boundaries' or 'The rules here don't allow me to do that' or any number of other similar comments.

On the surface, these are correct statements of fact, and the worker is using them to explain why a boundary crossing event can't happen. It is sometimes the quickest and easiest way to explain something to a client without annoying them and spoiling your relationship.

The problem is that these are essentially passive reactions that contain an implicit weakness. The client may well hear: 'Sorry, I can't do that because of professional boundaries, but if the rules were different then I would.' It could be interpreted as: 'I don't make the rules, I don't even like the rules, but I have to enforce them.'

For a vulnerable or manipulative client, this can be an invitation to continue to try to push the boundary to get what they want.

The fact that the worker is effectively hiding behind the rules rather than owning or explaining them means that the statement is more ambiguous, less confident and invites the client to think that there is some hope that their request might be met. It can sound like (and could even be true) the worker does not believe in the boundaries that they are enforcing.

Challenging inappropriate behaviour

There will be many occasions when clients will behave in ways that are unacceptable or inappropriate. For example, they might be:

- using inappropriate language

- insulting or disrespecting you

- breaking rules/agreed boundaries

- bullying other clients.

These types of behaviour have to be dealt with in some way by staff/workers. We have a duty of care to other clients and we need to maintain certain standards of behaviour in our projects/offices/ workplaces.

Most clients are aware when they or others are crossing boundaries or behaving inappropriately. If they act in this way in front of workers without any action in response, they will feel free to continue and to push more boundaries. If your project or workplace feels lawless and uncontrolled then it is much more likely that you will have serious incidents or problematic behaviour than if it is a boundaried environment.

However, we are not running schools or prisons, we don't have very many sanctions that we can use and we need to maintain a positive therapeutic relationship with our clients.

In most cases the only real sanction that we have is withdrawing the service that the client receives (ending their sessions or banning them from the project/service/offices). As we are working with vulnerable clients who are in need of help and may not have anywhere else to go, withdrawing a service is often a measure of last resort.

This means that we need to use our relationship with the clients and our communication skills to manage behaviour. In practice this means challenging the client about the behaviour and explaining to them why it is inappropriate.

If you simply shout at them, tell them off or reprimand them then you are likely to offend them or break any positive bond that you may have built up and you will not teach them anything. Ideally you should stop the behaviour, get them to think about the reasons that the behaviour is inappropriate, and suggest a different way of behaving.

There is no guaranteed method. Some clients have such deeply rooted self-defence mechanisms, or are not used to boundaries being imposed, that they are very sensitive. However, assertive communication skills and the following techniques of communicating boundaries to your clients will smooth over many issues.

Communicating boundaries to clients

There are four simple techniques that you can use to ensure that any of your responses are confident, assertive and that the client will take on board what you have to say. You can use them individually, all together, or one after another.

OWN YOUR STATEMENT

For example, 'I don't think that is appropriate behaviour,' and 'Sorry, I am not prepared to do that.'

By using 'I', you own the statement, which is both powerful and demonstrates that you personally care about the outcome.

EXPLAIN THE REASONS FOR THE BOUNDARY

'It is important that we keep the relationship on a professional level. It keeps us focused on the work and protects us both.'

'If I do all the work for you then you won't learn anything and you will become dependent on me.'

The explanation shows that you understand and believe in the reasons for the boundary but also helps the client understand your refusal.

FLIP IT BACK TO THE CLIENT

'Does the answer to that make any difference to your recovery?'

'What do you think will happen if I do that?'

This changes the dynamic of the situation and gets the client to think about the issue or think about themselves.

All of these responses are much stronger, confident and more assertive and are more likely to re-focus the client away from pushing at the boundary.

USE HUMOUR

If you can use it well and pull it off, then humour can help diffuse a situation or soften a message. It can get past people's defensiveness and get them to see the other side of a situation without it being thrust in their face.

However, do be careful – some people are better at it than others. If you mistime or misjudge a comment you will cause many more problems than you solve.

Dealing with manipulation

Most people manipulate situations and people to some extent or other. As workers we spend time trying to manipulate clients into behaving in certain ways (more healthily, more positively, more boundaried). Even on a very simple level most people would be nicer and more polite if they wanted something from someone, or might play up an injury if they wanted sympathy or play it down if they wanted to look brave or stoic.

Social care workers often do have a certain authority over their clients, or at the very least represent authority. We often have the ability to allow or deny clients access to services or resources that they want or they may require a report from or by us. If we work in a project or organisation there will be rules and boundaries to be enforced. Even a privately employed counsellor can come to represent a parental figure or someone whom the client wishes to impress.

This all means that we often have to deal with manipulative behaviour from our clients. Not all clients and not all the time, but it is important that you learn to spot and deal with manipulative clients.

Dealing with a manipulative client can be very challenging and tiring even for the most experienced worker. To be aware of when you are being manipulated can be difficult if the manipulator is very skilled.

Although it is difficult to manage, the solution is actually very simple: *maintain your boundaries*. If you stay on top of all your boundaries it will be very hard for a client to manipulate you. If you are assertive, don't treat them as a special case, don't bend the rules for them, maintain your boundaries of time and place, enforce all rules fairly and consistently, and maintain a professional (not personal) relationship, it will be very hard for them to manipulate you.

Once you start breaking or crossing boundaries you are either already being manipulated or you are leaving the door open for them to manipulate you.

Don't take it personally

It may be easier said than done, but it is important to keep in mind that you are doing a job and that most of what happens should not be taken too personally.

Clients can be difficult, frustrating, rude, upsetting and unpleasant at times. They can also be very nice, friendly, complimentary, grateful and uplifting. However your clients make you feel you must remember not to take it personally. You need to develop a thick professional skin to protect yourself.

If a client is kicking off, being obstructive or being rude or aggressive to you, it is very rarely a reaction to you personally. It is mostly because of what you represent, or the role that you are in, or because of frustrations in their own life. If you let their behaviour affect you on a personal level your work and your personal life will suffer.

If a client is being really nice or complimentary you could get too caught up in the praise and your ego can start to take over. This will also lead to broken boundaries and twisted priorities.

If a client is getting to you emotionally (positively or negatively) it can make it harder to manage a number of boundaries. Becoming upset or emotional makes us much more vulnerable to breaking boundaries ourselves as we also lose our professional detachment and objectivity.

There are a number of things you can do to avoid taking things personally as described below.

Look at the big picture

Step back from the situation and look at the bigger picture: What is it that you are trying to achieve with this client? How far have you come? What are the factors that make it difficult? What is your role? What interventions have you made? How are you going to move forward?

Whilst none of these questions may address what it is that is getting to you, looking at the big picture will put it into context and diminish its power.

Analyse the client's behaviour

Think about the client and what you know about them. Why are they behaving in the way that they are? As you spend time analysing their behaviour you will realise that the reasons for their behaviour are at root about themselves and not about you. Realising clearly that this is not about you helps de-personalise the situation.

Only take responsibility for what is yours

It is very easy when we become involved with a client to start to take on responsibility for their behaviour. Make sure that you are not doing this, since it will exhaust you and will make them dependent on you. At the end of the day we only control our own behaviour – everyone is responsible for themselves. Although you have a job to do to support your clients, you can only do so much. If they are not prepared to make the effort to change, you cannot make them change.

Have a look at the situation that you find yourself in. Have you acted in a professional and boundaried way and in the client's best interests? If you have, then anything after that is the client's responsibility and you should not take it on board. If you have not done this, then take responsibility for your action and do your best to change the way you work and move forward.

Acknowledge and accept your feelings

We can't control our feelings – we can only accept them. If what a client is saying or doing is impacting on you emotionally, don't ignore or suppress what you are feeling. It is important to acknowledge what you are feeling, but, having done so, don't let that feeling dominate your thoughts or your judgement.

Get support

Talking about an issue (within the bounds of confidentiality) helps to put things in perspective. If you feel that things are becoming a little personal then talk to a colleague or a manager about it.

Using supervision

One of the most useful things you can do to help yourself manage your boundaries is to discuss any issues in supervision or line management (assuming that you are lucky enough to have the right structures or the manager to allow you to do so). The chance to discuss and consider your issues with someone other than yourself is invaluable. Discuss issues early, as soon as you spot them, rather than waiting for them to become a problem.

Someone else's opinion is very valuable to set your work in context. You may find that you are exaggerating the problem in your own mind and someone else can see the bigger picture. It could also be that you have not realised the seriousness of the issue and speaking to someone else will help you realise what is really going on.

It can be difficult to discuss these issues because you are potentially discussing your mistakes or poor practice. It is easy to be embarrassed when talking about boundary issues. A good manager/supervisor will appreciate that you need a forum to discuss/explore your work practice. Most social care professionals step over the line at some time or other and there is no shame in admitting that you have made a mistake.

Assuming you have an reasonably understanding manager/supervisor, if you are unwilling to share your work practice with them, you will be setting up a very negative pattern of behaviour for yourself. The guilt/shame of holding back or hiding the problem will make dealing with the issue even harder. Once you have spoken about a difficult issue, it loses some of its power over you and it will be easier to move forward. There is also a strong chance that your clients will mirror or pick up on your secretive ways.

It is good practice to go to supervision/line management with an idea of what you want to talk about. Boundary issues can get forgotten, so make a note in a diary or notebook of issues that come up in between meetings.

Communicating

Communication is a very obvious but vital part of boundary management if you are working within a team. The more you communicate about boundaries and boundary issues, the more successful you will be at managing them.

Highlighting boundaries to clients

You should let your clients know, as often as possible, both the boundaries for their behaviour and the boundaries for what you will and won't do. Don't just do it verbally and don't think that a quick once-over upon induction is enough.

Boundary warnings to clients

If a client steps over a line you should let them know that the behaviour is inappropriate and remind them of the boundaries.

Forming a team response to clients breaking boundaries

If your fellow workers do not know what is going on for the clients who you jointly work with, or the clients who you exclusively work with, they will not be able to make informed decisions. The more you talk about your practice together, the easier it will be to work consistently together and the more you will be able to predict and trust each other's decisions.

Team discussions

It is always worth discussing boundaries with your team – the more you have a chance to thrash out difficult issues the more consistent your boundaries will be.

Boundary alerts to colleagues

If a particularly serious boundary is broken, or a client is prone to break particular boundaries, then let your colleagues know. They may well have to deal with the client and the more information that they have the better they will deal with them. A quick email, phone call or even shout round the office can save lots of work later.

Handover / debrief

If you have a handover/debrief system in place, make sure you use to it communicate any boundary issues that are going on in the organisation.

Discussing with managers

Anything which could have a serious implication for you, for the organisation or for other workers should be communicated to your manager as soon as possible. If a situation could leave you in a bad light, it is much better for your manager to hear it from you first.

Sharing information on boundary crossings with your manager not only protects you, but enables them to take decisions with the big picture in mind.

Personal into professional

One simple rule to help ensure you manage boundaries is to turn something personal into something professional. Often, by changing the context of a situation, what could be a boundary crossing action can be changed into boundaried behaviour.

Here are a few good examples of this in action, but mostly this requires a little thought on your part to come up with solutions that are relevant to your situation.

Gifts from clients

This example is common practice and well known but is a classic example of personal into professional. If a client offers you a gift, you can accept the gift 'on behalf of your team', making it clear that the gift will be shared, or donated to the staff Christmas raffle. This turns receiving a personal gift into something professional.

Books

It is quite common for workers to want to give or lend books to clients, for a variety of reasons (some professional, some personal). For a worker to give a book to a particular client is a personal action that should be avoided. However, if there is a shelf of books in the waiting room/reception/lounge that clients are entitled to take or borrow, the worker can donate the book to the shelf and then the client can have access to it.

'Just doing my job'

'I'm just doing my job' is a very simple phrase that can be used to deflect an overly eager or dependent client if they are praising you. It may be a clichéd phrase, but it takes a personal statement and reinterprets it as a professional one. It is quite important to remind yourself and your clients that this is a job that you do and that you are not sacrificing yourself out of the goodness of your heart.

You can use the same statement if someone is unhappy with you enforcing a rule or following procedure. However, in this situation this can be interpreted wrongly and come across as unassertive.

Attending events

As a worker you may be invited to attend celebrations or events by clients (graduations, award ceremonies, weddings, christenings). Some of these events may even bear some relation to the work you have been doing with the client. Going to the event on your own is quite a personal act and it can lead to a variety of problems. However, if you were able to attend with other members of staff and/or some clients you could make it a much more professional situation.

Funerals are a little different, if they are the funeral of one of your clients (not one of their relatives). However, in this case you would be there representing the service or in your role as worker.

If you are going to an event, do ensure that you stay for the main event only and don't attend any celebrations or socialising after the event.

Managing unavoidable dual relationships

There may be times when you are confronted with a service user who you have an existing relationship with and who you have an obligation to provide a service to. It is important that you ensure that the client has access to services – it would not be fair or reasonable to deny someone support because they are the cousin of a worker, or are employed by the manager of a service. As a worker, if you find that a client who is known to you in any way presents at the service, you should notify your manager immediately. Dual relationships can cause problems very quickly so don't delay.

Refer to another service

The simplest and easiest way to deal with the problem is to refer the client to another local service that can provide the same support. You should of course check that the location of the service and what they provide does meet the client's needs. Many services have geographical boundaries which define which clients they can see. It can be useful to set up a protocol between neighbouring services so that you can see clients from each other's area in extreme circumstances. If you work on your own, then knowing other local practitioners can help you set up similar support networks.

Managing the crossing within the organisation

If you provide a service in a more remote location or there are no other appropriate services within a reasonable distance, then you may have no choice but to work with a client with a dual relationship.

You then need to set up a number of special measures to try to limit the difficulties that may arise for you or the client.

Id you would arrange for the client to be seen by another worked set up arrangements that ensure that the worker with the dual ionship has limited access to information about the client.

should sit down with the client and talk through the potential diffies and explain what measures you have put in place to deal with the situation and explain how they should behave to help the sit on. It may be worth setting boundaries between the worker and the client about how they will deal with the situation outside o work.

If necessary and possible you can speak to other clients to bring e fact of the dual situation into the open and explain how it is eing dealt with. This can counter any suspicions of favouritism.

Questions to think about

- What are your high-risk situations? Look at situations where boundaries have been crossed in the past (personally or professionally). What was the build-up to the situation? What was going on for you at the time?

- How easy do you find it to be assertive? What sort of behaviour really winds you up? What situations do you lose your cool and get angry in? What sort of behaviour or what sort of people do you find it hard to stand up to?

Chapter 11

Self-awareness

Most social care workers rely to a great extent on the quality and the nature of the relationship that they have with their clients. To maintain this relationship on a professional level requires concentration and focus. However, our brains and personalities work on a subconscious level that we are not always aware of.

Our own experience of key relationships in our life affects our ability to form healthy relationships. How we have processed our own personal issues will all impact on how we work with clients. It is very easy to slip into old, or normal (for us), patterns of behaviour when working with clients. Without realising it we can start to act out our subconscious patterns and behaviour scripts. Because it is so easy to do, you need to be aware of your issues and patterns of behaviour, so that you can spot them when they arise.

There are many decisions about clients that hang on the balance between the client's desires and the client's best interests. This has to be judged by the worker, taking into account their own professional judgement. These decisions can be very tricky and quite emotive and require you to make a clear and objective decision. If some of your personal issues are particularly close to the surface when you are faced with the decision, it can be very hard to make the right choice.

Paradoxically, many of the reasons why individuals may be good at aspects of social work are the very things that can make them vulnerable to breaking boundaries. If you are a 'people-pleaser' (see below) you will be good at building rapport with people and good at understanding their needs and their moods. If you are strongly motivated by the death of a member of the family you will work hard and with a passion that will drive you. However, both these things can lead to broken boundaries.

There is nothing wrong with having needs, even with having what might be seen as 'dysfunctional' needs and issues. However, if you are going to support vulnerable people you need to make sure that you can leave your personal issues aside whilst at work.

To do this effectively you must do three things:

1. *Be aware what your needs and issues are.* Have a look at some of the ideas and theories contained in this chapter. Have a good, hard look at yourself and see if you recognise any patterns of behaviours. Many of these theories overlap and intertwine and you may recognise some pieces of the way you operate as an individual in different aspects of different theories. You don't need to label yourself, but it might help highlight some of your patterns of behaviour. You may find that you behave differently depending on the setting and the people you are interacting with.

2. *Ensure that your emotional needs are being met outside work.* Depending on how well you can separate and manage your feelings this can be done in various ways. It can be as simple as having a network of friends and relatives who support you or it could be as formal as having therapy and going to support groups. If you are unhappy or frustrated with your life, yourself or your situation, make sure that you take action to work on and improve this and don't let your work be the one thing that makes, or keeps, you happy.

3. *Monitor your own behaviour and feelings.* Make sure that you take time to reflect on yourself and how you work with clients, particularly if you identify any high-risk situations or any signs and symptoms of boundary crossings.

This may seem as if you are being asked to be perfect, to not have any issues or baggage and to live an exemplary life. We all have our own history and our own set of frailties and insecurities (even those who don't appear to and especially those who strenuously deny that they have any). This is what makes us who we are and gives us character and personality. What is being asked of you is that you have a level of understanding, so that you can recognise if things are getting out of control. You need to be able to be aware if you are focusing too much on your needs rather than those of the client.

Why do you want to do this job?

This simple but to-the-point question was asked to me by my first supervisor. At the time I wanted to learn about skills for working with clients and strategies to help them. For the first couple of sessions we talked about me. It turned out to be the most useful thing anyone ever taught me in social care.

What I came to realise over the course of those sessions was that my motivation for working in the field, what I was looking to get back, my 'pay-off', would affect how I worked with clients.

We all have different motivations for working in social care and we all get different things out of it. There are not many people who have chosen to work in the social care field because they hate it and don't get anything out of it. Many of us do the work because we get at least some of our needs met by helping or working with other people. It may be as simple as a sense of satisfaction from helping others, or a desire to do good, but we all get our pay-off somewhere along the line.

Take a minute to think about these questions in relation to the work that you do, or are training to do:

- What made you interested in the field or work or particular job?

- What do you enjoy about the job?

- How do you think you will feel at the end of a satisfying week at work?

- What will make you feel good about yourself?

- What would make you feel bad about yourself?

- How will all these things affect how you work with clients?

As the focus of our work, and our decision-making, should be focused around our clients' needs, it is important that we are able to identify and separate our own needs.

If you don't understand what your needs are it will be very hard to identify them. If you can't identify them then you will be in danger of basing decisions on your needs, not your clients' needs.

Ending the relationship

Worker: Ben, a housing support worker who likes to support people

Client: Clive, a former rough sleeper who is now in his own flat

Ben and Clive have been working together for four months, Clive is doing really well settling into his flat, managing his bills and starting a new life. He is doing better than most other clients that Ben is working with and they both get along really well.

Their time working together is due to end in two months' time and Clive is due to move on to a floating support service. He tells Ben that he really values the support that Ben has given him and that no one else really understands him the way Ben does. Ben feels good about the work he is doing and is glad to be of support. He feels needed and pleased with himself.

As the time to end the relationship approaches, Clive starts becoming slightly less organised and together. He is not managing his tenancy and himself quite as well as he had been previously. He tells Ben that he would like to extend the relationship for another three months so that he can get himself sorted out. He tells Ben what a great worker he is and how he could never have got this far without him.

Ben's policies allow him to extend the relationship in 'exceptional circumstances'.

If Ben extends his time with Clive, he may be just reinforcing Clive's dependency on him. If he ends the relationship now it could have a bad affect on Clive. It is a difficult decision, and Ben needs to make sure that his ego does not interfere with weighing up the pros and cons.

People-pleasing

This is a very common trait and a term that is in common usage. A people-pleaser will want everyone to like them and will be very concerned that everyone else is happy. Generally a people-pleaser will be very empathic and will be able to judge quickly how to act to ingratiate themselves with someone else.

People-pleasing commonly develops as a defence mechanism to avoid rejection or disapproval. A people-pleaser will hate other people to be angry about or towards them.

As a result, people-pleasers can be easy to manipulate, particularly if the other person is aggressive, moody or distant. People-pleasers can also have difficulty setting boundaries and are more likely to bend rules for people or be a 'soft touch' and may not like challenging clients.

The following is a list of stereotypical traits of people-pleasers:

- Having trouble saying no to people.

- Silently putting up with other people's behaviour even if it upsets you.

- Feeling better about yourself when supporting other people.

- Only feeling happy when those close to you are happy.

- Doing more than your share at home or at work.

- Feeling love towards people who you can help or rescue.

- Feeling bad if you speak up for yourself.

- Working hard to avoid arguments or confrontations.

- Being concerned what other people think of you.

- Smiling and laughing when you feel down.

- Feeling rejected when people close to you have other significant relationships.

- Having difficulty expressing what you really feel to other people.

- Having trouble accepting compliments.

- Having difficulty expressing anger.

- Feeling personal shame when people you look after make mistakes.

- Thinking that people close to you would not be able to cope without you.

- Feeling that other people should put more effort in to help you.

- Not being able to say no if people ask you for help.

- Having difficulty saying yes when you are offered help.

Co-dependency

Co-dependency is a concept that was originally developed by Alcoholics Anonymous. It started as a fairly simple concept but has taken on a life of its own and there are many interpretations of exactly what it is. Here we do not discuss the wider debate about co-dependency, but will just look at a few key aspects as they relate to professional care workers.

The theory centres around the idea of a mutual dependency between those who need support and those who give it. Someone who suffers from co-dependency will have trouble forming healthy and balanced relationships and may look to other people or other things to sustain their feelings of self-worth.

Typically, someone who is co-dependent would sacrifice their needs to support others and would derive their self-worth from this sacrifice. They only feel good about themselves when the people who they 'care' for are feeling good. As the carer needs to feel needed they subconsciously want the 'patient' to remain dependent on them. This disempowers the 'patient' and sets up a cycle of dependency. Initially it may seem that the person who is 'sick' and needs caring for is dependent on the carer, but this can soon change.

A co-dependent individual may act the 'martyr', voluntarily giving up their time and energy and feeling unthanked and unappreciated when they are not valued enough in return. They may also work really hard to meet other people's needs, but not be able to ask for what they want. They expect others to guess or intuit what they want and need and feel resentful when the others do not.

Co-dependency can appear in family relationships, amongst friends or between workers and clients. It is classically seen in the family and friends of people with addiction problems, mental health issues or long-term physical health issues.

It is essentially a passive aggressive behaviour and is based on low self-esteem, not feeling that your rights are worth asserting and working harder and harder to please other people in the hope that they will respect your rights and needs.

You will also find that co-dependents will often indulge in other self-destructive behaviours, such as gambling, addictions, eating disorders and workaholism.

We work in a field that involves supporting and working with vulnerable people and it is certainly likely to attract a high proportion of co-dependents as both workers and clients. Many people who work in social care do so because of some personal experience, either of the issues involved, or by proxy through family members and friends.

The dependent

The other side of co-dependency is those people who like having someone running around after them and looking after their needs. Stereotypically, narcissists are more likely to be clients than workers, but there is still a strong cross-over.

The dependent will rely strongly on other people to be able to perform certain tasks, will find change difficult, will enjoy being 'in charge', will find it much easier to spot other people's problems than their own and will enjoy pointing them out to others.

The dependent will like being flattered and having their ego massaged and won't take criticism or feedback well. The dependent is also likely to indulge in self-destructive behaviours. They will be very good at building rapport quickly, will have a strong, noticeable personality, but may have difficulty in maintaining long-term friendships.

The dependent worker will find it difficult when clients do not follow their advice and may take any rejection by clients very badly. It is also possible that their pride, ego and vanity may get in the way of decision-making.

Personal experience

Many people working in social care are there because of personal experience – either direct personal experience of some related issues, or experience of a family member, partner or close friend who has suffered from those issues. This experience can bring passion, dedication and a depth of feeling to a role that is hard to match. However, it can also cause problems.

Some workers may want to set things right or fix things for others that they were unable to do in their own life, for themselves or others. Others may support other people in an effort to rewrite or change situations that they have experienced. Some may just want to share their experience and turn what could have been a negative experience into one for good.

This can lead to a number of problems, made more likely because of the strength of feeling that it may evoke and because it can key into significant life experiences.

The closeness of the subject can mean that the worker becomes less objective. Personal experiences and emotions can start to colour judgement on key issues, drawing up old and deep feelings, which can be powerful enough to destabilise the worker and leading to the worker over-identifying with the clients, creating a special bond in either the mind of the worker, the client or both. This can lead to flawed decisions, special treatment and blurred boundaries.

Over-identifying

Ginny's father was an alcoholic and drank himself into an early grave when she was ten years old. Ginny was too young to be able to help her father and after he died felt very guilty that she had been unable to save him. As an adult she ended up working as a nurse in an alcohol detox unit.

There are certain clients who remind Ginny of her father, and she goes out of her way to look after these clients, spending more time with them, making sure they are ok and bending the rules for them on occasions.

The centre has strict entry requirements but Ginny is prone to admitting clients who are not entirely suitable if they remind her of her father.

Other people's problems

Other people's problems are always easier to solve than your own. Identifying, fixing and solving other people's problems makes you feel good about yourself. It saves having to look at your own issues and problems. Looking at the difficulties that other people face and the situations that they get themselves into makes you feel better about your life. Coming to work can be a relief, an escape from your own problems into a world of other people's problems.

Fixers

Many people in the social care sector want to fix things for people, to make things right or undo the impact of injustices or unfairness in the world. This urge can also extend into wanting to make people feel happier or better about themselves.

A fixer finds it hard to accept other people's distress. The desire to make things better can lead to the individual taking on responsibility for others' happiness or success.

Fixers will absorb other people's feelings and energies and will therefore be very affected by those around them. Fixers will pick up on other people's feelings and will take those feelings on as their own.

This means that fixers not only become entangled with their clients' emotions very easily but also that they start to take too much responsibility for the way that their clients feel, and this will disempower the clients.

Questions to think about

If you look at Cognitive Behavioural theory you can see very clearly that our personal desires and beliefs about ourselves and others drive our actions. How we act is picked up on by others and they will respond accordingly. We will therefore attract people who find a fit with our personality. If you want to look after people, this will be expressed in your actions; people who want to be looked after will pick up on this (consciously and subconsciously) and latch on to you. If you are controlling and egotistical this will also come through in your actions and you will attract people who want others to make decisions for them.

- What are the messages that you give out?

- What sort of people do you attract, and why?

Appendix I

Useful Organisations

UK organisations

Care Quality Commission

www.cqc.org.uk

The CQC regulates care provided by the NHS, local authorities, private companies and voluntary organisations in hospitals, care homes and people's own homes. The website contains guidance, reports and regulations.

Clinic for Boundary Studies

www.professionalboundaries.org.uk

An excellent organisation, which provides information, training and support. They work with particular focus on preventing abuse and supporting clients who have been abused.

Community Care Magazine

www.communitycare.org.uk

The website of an excellent magazine aimed at social workers. It contains excellent articles and an active forum that has good discussions about all aspects of social work practice.

Department of Communities and Local Government

www.communities.gov.uk

This website contains government guidance and policy for the housing sector. There is a very detailed Quality Assessment Framework which was issued as part of Supporting People Guidance. Whilst the funding and reporting framework around Supporting People has changed, the standards are still in place and continue to be very detailed and comprehensive professional standards.

Department of Health

www.dh.gov.uk

This website contains a wealth of material relating to laws, regulations and guidance for all areas of social care.

General Social Care Council
www.gscc.org.uk
The GSCC is the body that sets standards of conduct and practice for social care workers and their employers in England, and maintains the Social Care Register. There is a good code of practice for social workers available on their website.

National Treatment Agency for Substance Misuse
www.nta.nhs.uk
The NTA produces a range of guidance for doctors, nurses, pharmacists, psychologists, consultant psychiatrists and other staff who provide treatment to drug misusers.

Sitra
www.sitra.org.uk
This website provides guidance on policy and standards in the housing and supported housing sector.

International organisations

American Counseling Association
www.counseling.org
The ACA promotes the counselling profession through work in advocacy, research and professional standards.

Australian Association of Social Workers
www.aasw.asn.au
Another excellent code of ethics is available from the AASW, though this is being reviewed in consultation with the organisation's members.

Australian Counselling Association
www.theaca.net.au
The ACA is primarily concerned with national registration, industry standards, and creating employment for counsellors.

Canadian Association of Social Workers
www.casw-acts.ca
The CASW also has an excellent code of ethics on its website, plus very useful guidelines for practice.

Canadian Counselling and Psychotherapy Association
www.ccacc.ca
The CCPA is a national and bilingual organisation dedicated to the enhancement of the counselling profession in Canada.

National Association of Social Workers
www.socialworkers.org/pubs/code/code.asp
The NASW is the largest social work union in the United States and has an excellent and comprehensive code of ethics available on their website.

Appendix II

Further Reading

Department of Health (2000) *'No Secrets': Guidance on Developing Multi-Agency Policies and Procedures to Protect Vulnerable Adults from Abuse.* Available at www.dh.gov.uk/en/Publicationsandstatistics/Lettersandcirculars/Healthservicecirculars/DH_4003726, accessed on 23 November 2011.

Guthiel, T.G. and Brodsky, A. (2008) *Preventing Boundary Violations in Clinical Practice.* New York: Guilford Press. An excellent book that goes deeper into the psychology of boundary crossings and violations.

Malin, N. (ed.) (2001) *Professionalism, Boundaries and the Workplace.* London: Routledge. A good general look at a number of boundary issues.

Rogers, C. (1961) *On Becoming a Person: A Therapist's View of Psychotherapy.* London: Constable.

Useful websites

Common law
http://webarchive.nationalarchives.gov.uk/+/www.dh.gov.uk/en/publicationsandstatistics/publications/publicationspolicyandguidance/browsable/DH_5803173

Information Commissioner
www.ico.gov.uk

Releasing information to prevent or detect crime
www.ico.gov.uk/upload/documents/library/data_protection/detailed_specialist_guides/section_29_gpn_v1.pdf

Mental Health Act 1983/Sectioning
www.mind.org.uk/help/rights_and_legislation/mental_health_act_1983_an_outline_guide

Mental capacity and the law
www.direct.gov.uk/en/Governmentcitizensandrights/Mentalcapacityandthelaw/index.htm

Index